This Won't Change Your Life

(But It Might Help!)

Elizabeth Pitman

CHANNEL VIEW BOOKS
Clevedon • Philadelphia

Dedication

This book is dedicated to my nieces, Kirsty and Sara, with love and appreciation

6003523380

British Library Cataloguing in Publication Data

Pitman, Elizabeth 1940–
This Won't Change Your Life (But It Might Help!)
1. Man. Behaviour.
I. Title
150

ISBN 1-873150-00-8

Channel View Books
An imprint of Multilingual Matters Ltd

Bank House, 8a Hill Road,   &   1900 Frost Road, Suite 101,
Clevedon, Avon BS21 7HH,   Bristol, PA 19007,
England.   USA.

Typeset by Editorial Enterprises, Torquay.
Printed and bound in Great Britain by the Longdunn Press, Bristol.

Contents

Preface

Not *Another* Book about Behaviour

There are already a number of books on aspects of behaviour—how to understand people, and vice versa; stop loving too much or too little; make better love; be more assertive and so on. Why another?

This book doesn't take a specialist approach, such as how to be more assertive; instead, it presents a more general approach to understanding everyday behaviour and communication. Although there are many theories about human behaviour, they are often complex and difficult to use in day-to-day life, and, to help us make sense of our emotional world, we often tend to fall back on common sense. Yet this can let us down badly when we are faced with difficulties in our work, family lives, or social situations. As a result, we may become distressed, stressed, and unhappy and feel unable to cope. While there are no magic solutions or panaceas for the emotional stresses of difficult work situations, unhappy marriages, and so on, this book is based on the view that there are, nevertheless, some relatively simple but constructive ideas about understanding and, if necessary, changing behaviour that can be used in everyday living.

If It's Not for Specialists, Then Who is It For?

It is intended primarily for people who are new or relatively new to theories of behaviour and for people who are curious about why we behave as we do. It should also be of interest to people who want to make some changes in themselves or their relationships, or who want to develop

1

options for managing difficult situations more effectively. Thus, it is mainly intended for the person who is in general getting on with life but who might like to be more effective and/or to make changes in some aspects of feelings, attitudes or behaviour. As such, it does not address issues of very deep emotional distress.

Whilst not specifically written for people who work in a helping role, social workers, counsellors, doctors, nurses and so on might also find this book useful as many of the ideas and exercises could be used with their clients or patients. It is not my intention to persuade you that once you've read this book life will necessarily always be stress and trauma free; it is intended as a useful guide to understanding personality, communication and behaviour, rather than as a complete answer to the problems of living.

So What Theories are Being Used?

This book is based on some of the ideas to be found in the theory of *transactional analysis*—a framework for understanding human behaviour which was originally developed by Eric Berne, who first became known through his best seller *Games People Play*. Transactional analysis explains how and why:

- our personalities develop as they do
- we communicate with varying degrees of effectiveness
- we behave in a variety of ways in order to get our needs met
- we develop the beliefs we hold.

It also provides ideas about changing attitudes and behaviour in relationships and situations in which we feel unhappy. It should not be regarded as a cure-all and it cannot, in itself, resolve major health, social or economic difficulties. Neither can it be used as a stick with which to beat other people who are not doing what we would like them to do.

There are many books on transactional analysis. Some provide in-depth accounts of its theory and practice and this makes them fairly inaccessible for the person who is new to theories of behaviour. Others provide a more popular introduction but can be somewhat over enthusiastic in their claims for how transactional analysis can change lives. I find in my training and counselling work that this rather evangelical approach can be off-putting to people; hence a basic beginner's guide, which it is hoped is neither over-enthusiastic nor evangelical, to some of the ideas in transactional analysis theory and practice.

The ideas put forward in this book are based on the work of a number of eminent writers on transactional analysis. In order to provide a clear and easily understood text I have in general avoided quotations and references to specific writers. My debt to these other writers is enormous and can only be partly acknowledged by their inclusion in the references for further reading given at the end.

Traditional transactional analysis theory uses a number of words in a very specialised sense. Sometimes this can seem like unnecessary and confusing jargon, and can be off-putting for people who are new to the subject. I have therefore used as few specialist or jargon words as possible, but an appendix contains a glossary of the conventional transactional analysis words and links them in with the words used in the main text.

Where does Transactional Analysis Fit with Other Theories of Behaviour?

There are today many theories and schools of thought about personality and behaviour. Some practitioners adhere faithfully to one particular school, such as that developed by Sigmund Freud. Others take a mix-and-match approach, taking ideas from a variety of sources. Sometimes the theories themselves seem to be a mixture of ideas from a range of sources, and transactional analysis, in my view, does this very successfully. It is broadly humanistic in its philosophical base, psychoanalytic in its concern with the way the past influences us in the present, but behaviourist in its emphasis on encouraging people to change as rapidly as possible.

Research into transactional analysis is still relatively limited, although what has been done has generally produced positive results. My own belief in the value of transactional analysis is based on its value in my own life, as well as several years' experience in teaching and counselling work. It has been helpful, both to many of the people with whom I have worked and myself, in enabling us to have a better understanding of normal behaviour, as well as helping us to clarify and resolve problems.

How Will the Ideas be Presented?

Each chapter covers an aspect of theory and concludes with a short exercise or questionnaire which can be used, both to help deepen understanding of theory and as a starting point for making changes. Chapter 11 then brings together the material found throughout the book and gives more detailed exercises with a focus on making changes.

I have alternated he and she throughout the text, in order to avoid sexual bias, as well as using the words counselling and therapy interchangeably. When I talk about parents, or parental influences, I am referring not only to actual parents, but also to other people, such as step-parents or social workers, who take on a parenting role.

As well as examples from my own experience, I have provided brief case examples as cameos to illustrate the ideas being presented. These are based on real situations from my counselling practice. Although permission has been given for these examples to be included, I have changed names for the sake of confidentiality.

Acknowledgements

I would like to thank Margaret Harris for her patient typing of an early draft, as well as Jean Thie and friends who read and commented on the script. My thanks also go to Ted Sparkes for his helpful suggestions on the text, patient editing and creative cartoons. Finally, I wish to thank the students and clients with whom I have worked over the years. Their enthusiasm for transactional analysis as an approach to understanding human behaviour has encouraged my own learning and increased my understanding.

CHAPTER 1

Getting to Know You

Knowing others is wisdom; knowing the self is enlightenment (Lao Tsu)

The ideas being presented in this book provide a blueprint that can help us understand ourselves both when things are going well and when the going gets tough. Unlike a blueprint from which machines are made, ours needs to include historical information about childhood experiences before it can provide a clear picture of the present. This chapter, then, gives a summary of the blueprint being presented in the book as a whole.

An Introduction to Childhood

Even before we are born, we need good physical care from our mothers. The woman who takes care of herself in terms of rest, relaxation, diet, and so on is more likely to give birth to a healthy and contented baby than the woman who is stressed or unable to have adequate rest, who smokes or drinks heavily, or has a poor diet. Once we are born, our very existence depends on the care we receive. Without adequate food, warmth and physical care, we soon die. Without love or emotional warmth and care, we can, in a sense, die emotionally or, at the very least, become very emotionally starved.

When we are young, our personalities are moulded by a complicated mixture of our inborn characteristics, such as our genes, instincts, and physiology; the physical care we receive in the form of food, warmth and the environment in which we live; and the emotional care given by our parents and other people. As we grow up, the ways in which we react to and deal with experiences may, to some extent, alter these early influences but they never completely obliterate them.

Emotional Hungers Need Meeting, Too

Because we need love as much as we need food, this need can be seen as a hunger, not unlike physical hunger. When we are very small, this is met by the stimulation and attention we receive from our parents. Some parents are well able to meet their children's needs by giving them lots of attention and affection, both in words and gestures. Their children are cuddled and made to feel lovable, attractive, talented and important. Alternatively, people who did not receive good parenting themselves may find it difficult to give their children the love and attention they need. Their children are rarely cuddled, or are told that they weren't wanted, or that they are ugly or stupid, or they may even be physically ill-treated, ignored or rejected.

Statements such as 'mummy loves you', 'you're daddy's pretty little girl', 'little boys don't cry' tell us, not only how our parents feel about us, but also their expectations of us. Although we may ignore these, many are incorporated and become the basis for our own particular blueprint. Sometimes we swallow them whole. 'Daddy's little girl' may either not marry, but remain rather immature, or she may marry, but find herself disappointed when her husband fails to be as adoring and attentive as her father was. Sometimes we re-interpret the expectation, turning a negative statement into a positive one, and vice versa. A child who decides that if 'little boys don't cry' big boys can, may well grow up to be more in touch with his feelings than a child who decides that if 'little boys don't cry', big boys can't either.

Ann grew up in a home where her mother was bringing up two children by herself. Her mother was stressed and depressed, and Ann came to believe that, even though she was still a little girl, her mother wanted her to take care of her. She began to feel responsible for making her mother happy, and used to try all sorts of ways to achieve this, although somehow it was never enough. Ann grew up transferring her feelings towards her mother to other situations. She felt over-responsible for other people, and spent a good deal of time looking after them, while still feeling this was never enough. She then became depressed and worn out herself. In therapy, as Ann made links between her present behaviour and her childhood, she began to let go of this need to take so much care of others. She still cared for others when it was appropriate, but she also learnt to pay more attention to what she wanted. As a result, she made major career decisions, changing from social work to photography, which allowed her to use far more of her untapped creative potential. She also developed friendships which were happier and more fulfilling and began to look after her physical self—eating and drinking more moderately and ensuring she didn't become so physically and emotionally exhausted by others' demands on her.

Developing Childhood Potential

Although part of the process of growing up is a case of responding to parental expectations and the 'dos' and 'don'ts' that parents impose, as children we spend much of our time having fun playing and being creative. We also learn to put 'two and two together' and to develop our capacity to think. We realise that the red shape fits into the red block, but the yellow shape doesn't, or that if we touch the stove when it's hot, we'll get burnt. Our conversation is full of questions and the answers we get should help us to understand the world around us, to work out problems, to think and to make decisions. Later in childhood, we begin to learn about looking after other people. For example, when my little niece began to cry because I'd been cross with her for running into the road, it was her older sister who first gave her a cuddle and said, 'Don't cry ... Aunty Liz isn't really cross—she was only afraid you'd get hurt'.

Finally, we develop a set of values in relation to ourselves and other people. When children write to world leaders with their fears about nuclear war, and their wish for peace, they are basing their pleas on their values about how they think the world should be.

Thus, as young children we have a capacity for fun and creativity, for thinking for ourselves, for taking care of others and ourselves and for developing a set of values and opinions. As we grow up, we make decisions, although not always consciously, in response to the experiences we had in early childhood, the expectations that people had of us and the way we developed our own capacities. These decisions then come to influence how we feel about ourselves, others and the world around us.

People whose childhood was, in general, happy and secure, are likely to believe that they are lovable, that they can trust other people and that the world is an interesting and exciting place. People who were neglected, rejected or abused in childhood are likely, unless they have been able to make some new decisions based on later and happier experiences and relationships, to believe that they are unlovable, or doomed to unhappiness, that they can't trust others and that the world is a dull and fearful place.

These early decisions and beliefs also influence the way we behave, the way we talk to and respond to others, and the way we spend our time. People who feel good about themselves are able to form close and loving relationships and to enjoy their own and others' company, as well as using their talents to the full. They are able to have fun and to enjoy life, as well as being competent and responsible in their work, relationships and so on. People who feel bad about themselves are liable to spoil relationships, to find their own and others' company difficult to cope with, and to misuse or abuse their talents. They could find it difficult to have fun or to enjoy life, and may well feel—or be—incompetent and irresponsible or ruthlessly competitive in their work, relationships and so on.

Life as a Business Organisation?

We are all, in fact, rather like a business organisation. We receive lots of inputs (attention, recognition, information about others' expectations of us). We then have to decide how to develop the business (personality, attitudes, feelings), and how to behave towards our colleagues (decisions, beliefs, behaviour). Finally, we send out salespeople, information or goods (communication, the way we spend our time, behaviour). In life, as in business, we may be successful (liking ourselves, fully developing our talents and skills) or we may break even (living safely, but dully) or even go bankrupt (making a mess of our lives, going crazy, killing ourselves).

Also, in life, as in business, our fortune is not entirely in our hands: sometimes, we crash because of factors beyond our control (accidents, ill-health, bereavement, unemployment); sometimes we never seem to have the chance to get off the ground (being born into poor or disadvantaged circumstances). But sometimes our business failure arises from our own attitudes (blaming others inappropriately when things go wrong, deciding that there is nothing we can do about the problems we face, or choosing to feel depressed, rather than challenged, by difficulties).

The ideas in this book are based on the belief that many of the difficulties in our attitudes, feelings and behaviour can be understood and resolved. I do not want to jump on the 'being perfect' bandwagon that seems to be both a part of our culture and of some psychological theories. Books, magazines, advertising and so on can seem to imply that we should all be aiming for perfection—the perfect figure, looks, fitness, marriage, personality, home and so on—and our inability to meet these dreams and expectations can encourage a sense of failure and discontentment. Change may be exciting, essential or useful, and it should help us to like ourselves as '*good enough*',[1] rather than perfect, people. The focus in this book is, therefore, on understanding yourself and others and on learning to like yourself 'warts and all'.

Getting Started

Begin with a fantasy ... imagine your present life as a business concern. Imagine what kind of business it might be, whether it is working as you would want it to be, or whether you might want to make changes.

Do you want to run a small show with just a few people, or do you want to go for the big time with lots of people around? Do you want to go for security or risk or a bit of both? Do you appreciate and fully use the resources you already have available? If your business is working just as you would wish, do you need to do anything to ensure it goes on running smoothly? If you feel it needs a shakeup, can you identify what it needs? How far might you be able to find the resources it needs? Are there some factors beyond your control you simply have to accept?

By asking yourself these questions in an imaginative way, you can, if you wish, begin to identify whether there are changes you might want to make in your work, your personal relationships, your attitudes, your goals and so on, or whether you simply want to sit back and savour your life as it is at present.

CHAPTER 2
Attention Please

We do not see things as they are. We see them as we are (The Talmud)

The Need for Attention

When a friend greets you with a hug and tells you how lovely it is to see you; when your partner buys you a specially chosen gift; when your child draws a picture especially for you, or a colleague tells you that a piece of work you have just finished is very good, you are receiving positive *recognition*, or *attention* from others.

We all need to feel that we are of value to ourselves and other people, and our sense of self needs affirming. Indeed, our emotional well-being is very much bound up with how well we and others meet our needs for recognition. This recognition occurs in the form of feedback, or acknowledgement, from others as well as the internal conversations we have with ourselves. It can be done in words or gestures—or both.

Although we all vary in our preferred pattern for giving and receiving such attention, depending on our backgrounds and lifestyles, there is—as long as we are satisfied with it—no right or wrong pattern. I enjoy the act of creative writing, which means that I need to be able to work enjoyably alone at home, whereas my brother, who is in business, enjoys spending much of his time meeting new people, and the excitement of competing for business. Patterns change, too, at different times in our lives. My sister-in-law has just taken the plunge back into work, becoming an aromatherapist after several years of being a full-time mother. She is finding the appreciation she receives from her newly relaxed and de-stressed clients both exciting and rewarding.

This need for recognition stems from our very earliest childhood. When we are born we require, not only food, warmth and shelter but stimulation and loving attention from our parents. We need them to show their love by physical contact, as well as by providing us with an emotionally nurturing climate in which to grow. Without such a relationship, it is difficult for us to grow up as emotionally healthy people. As we grow older, the amount of physical contact we get from others usually decreases, and we need to develop more strongly other ways of meeting our needs for recognition and attention. As adults, we receive this acknowledgement from others in the form of loving words and actions, compliments, information, criticism and so on, as well as in smiles, hugs and kisses.

Most of us, whether we live with other people or on our own would, in a typical week, have a considerable amount of contact with a wide range of people. These contacts vary in intensity and intimacy, but might include such things as going to work and seeing colleagues, having a cup of tea with a neighbour, collecting children from school, having a meal with the family, or meeting friends in the evening. We would probably be involved in talking about work, hearing about the school or work day, discussing mutual friends, interests, politics and so on. Most of us would find it difficult to cope if the people we love and care about, or even the people with whom we are less intimately involved, but with whom we have some kind of contact, stopped acknowledging us.

Imagine, for a moment, a typical week in your own life. Think about the contacts you have with people, and the kind of things you do together. Now imagine that, in this week all the people whom you consider as important to you ignore you completely, so that you come to feel that you are invisible.

What would be your reaction to this? Would it be a relief to have a break from the daily demands of your life, or would you feel anxious? Would you be quite happy about this invisibility, or would you feel uncared for? Although some people feel the need for a good deal of solitude, most of us would, I suspect, feel some discomfort during this imaginary week. We are, in general, very social creatures, relying on each other for emotional support as well as for our more practical day to day needs, and the total isolation of such invisibility would usually prove both difficult and distressing.

Different Kinds of Attention

The kind of recognition and attention we give to each other varies in both type and intensity. It can range from comparatively superficial attention through caring friendships, to the intimacy involved in close and loving marriages and partnerships.

The following greeting probably occurs hundreds of times in this or similar form every day:

'Good morning. How are you? Awful weather isn't it?'
'Good morning. Fine thanks. Yes, terrible—I'm fed up with it.'

Although you might not feel very satisfied if all your contacts were as brief and superficial as this, these kinds of exchanges can help you to feel valued, as well as rooted in your immediate environment. If you should move to a new town, these rather superficial daily contacts can be of particular importance in helping you to feel at home, and can on occasions be the forerunners of deeper, more lasting friendships.

If you spend a relaxed and happy evening with someone, you are involved in giving and receiving a much deeper form of recognition. While the kind and amount of closeness will vary, depending on what is happening in your life at any particular time, you will probably feel the need for loving relationships with others. And though these relationships often occur within the family, the emphasis on romantic and exclusive love in our culture tends to mean that we under-value the affection and concern we can give to and receive from friends, neighbours

Have a nice day

and colleagues. Whether or not close family links form part of your day-to-day life, good friendships can also be a valuable source of recognition from others.

Positive Attention is Best

The best kind of attention you can receive from others is that which enhances your sense of yourself as unique, special and lovable. Such attention doesn't have any strings attached to it. You don't have to do anything to get it—just simply be yourself. When you say, or have said to you:

> 'I love you'
> 'I think you're great'
> 'I like being with you'

you are giving or receiving *positive*, *unconditional recognition* or *attention*.

Sometimes the attention is just as positive, but not as all-embracing and is more to do with what you do rather than with how you are. It thus provides good, but more limited recognition. As a child, this would have encouraged you to behave according to your parents' expectations. By doing so, you not only kept their love, but also learnt to get along in a world in which consideration for other people plays a not-unimportant part. As an adult, this more specific and limited recognition gives you useful feedback about how others see you, and about your abilities. Comments such as:

> 'That's a great tie you're wearing'
> 'That report was very well done'
> 'I like your sense of humour'

are examples of *positive, conditional attention.*

Positive recognition can also be given in actions. Giving a smile, a hug, a gift; careful listening when someone is sharing a problem; preparing a favourite meal for a friend, all demonstrate positive regard and recognition.

Positive does not of course simply mean affirmative recognition about your qualities and talents. In order to learn new skills, or to make changes in your attitudes or behaviour, or to sustain a good relationship over a long period of time, you sometimes need to accept comments about some aspects of your work or yourself. Because these comments are about making changes in the way you do your work, and so on, they are normally seen as being critical. Few of us like adverse criticism, but it is important to make a clear distinction between negative, destructive criticism, and positive, constructive criticism. Unfortunately, because it is perhaps often given in an angry or hostile manner, criticism has come to be seen as a negative thing, rather than something that can be helpful.

If critical feedback is given in a genuine and constructive way, and if it enhances aspects of your personality or behaviour, it is an aspect of positive recognition. It is important for such feedback to give clear information about what can be done in order for changes to be made. If done lovingly, such feedback can result in more openness and honesty between people, and can help, rather than hinder relationships. It can also give you ideas about how to develop your talents and skills more effectively.

I realise that this whole area of positive, critical feedback is a minefield. All too often, feedback is given because the giver thinks it will be good for the person receiving it. What it can really mean is that we are attempting to impose our own standards and values on others. While this is necessary in some cases, if we are to live together in some sort of civilised society, telling people things 'for their own good' is fraught with difficulty. Positive critical feedback really does need to be for the well-being of the person receiving it, and not merely for the good of the person giving it. It also needs to be done sparingly and with great sensitivity and care.

Attention is Positive Only When it's Sincere

Sometimes, apparently positive recognition is really only sugar-coating for negative attention. Giving someone a perfunctory peck whilst looking at the television news over his shoulder is not really positive recognition. Saying to a friend 'Dar...ling, what a beautiful dress, I had one just like it last year' is a statement with a very real sting in the tail. If you feel a degree of discomfort when receiving an apparently positive statement or action, it might be that you are, in fact, getting *insincere negative attention*, or recognition which can be seen as *plastic*, rather than real.

Negative Attention Can Hurt

Although some critical feedback can be constructive, if people say things to you that are intended to be hurtful, then you are getting negative attention. Sometimes, because you are feeling tired, unhappy, or hurt, you might give negative attention to people you like. This can also be all-embracing, or more specific and limited. Saying:

> 'I hate you'
> 'You bore me'
> 'You're stupid'

are examples of *unconditional negative attention*. At times the negative feedback might not be as all-embracing, but it is still unhelpful and possibly hurtful, rather than constructive. Comments such as:

> 'You're a lousy cook'
> 'You've made a real mess of that'
> 'Do you call that tidying up your room'

are examples of *conditional negative recognition*. While more specific, they are still negative and potentially hurtful, rather than constructive, ways of giving critical feedback.

Some examples of negative recognition given in actions might be a slap; a pointed, wagging finger; deliberately ignoring someone; constant interrupting when being told something.

Few of us like getting negative attention, but we can choose how to deal with it when we do get it. It is as important to be able to reject, ignore or to challenge negative attention, as it is to accept positive attention. It is worth bearing in mind that 'sticks and stones can break your bones, but names can't hurt you'. If a friend tells you that your new hair style doesn't suit you as well as the old one, you can say that though she may not like it, you do and you're glad you've had it done. If your boss says that the report you've just handed him was no good, you can ask calmly for the reasons and for suggestions for improving it.

Asking for Attention

Sometimes if you're unsure about a piece of work you've done, you're feeling tired, or have had a difficult day, you may feel you'd like some positive attention. You may, of course, find it difficult to ask in a direct and open way for the support or love you feel you need, or think that if you have to ask for it, it loses its value, or that having asked you still might not get it. You may then find that, even though you haven't been clear about what you need, you become resentful or angry when it isn't forthcoming.

Many of us have what I call the crystal ball expectation, believing that, if the people we care about really loved us, they would always know when we were unhappy, tired, or fed up.

We therefore expect or hope that the people whom we most want attention from will provide it without being asked. Obviously, because other people do not have a crystal ball, or may themselves be tired, stressed or pre-occupied, there are times when this doesn't happen.

When I first met Lisa, she felt that other people only saw her as being efficient, confident and competent, but ignored the fact that she felt, at times, uncertain, let down, upset or angry.

Instead of being open about her feelings and her needs for support and affection from her friends, she hoped people would see beneath the efficient exterior and respond to her less-secure self. She became angry and depressed inside when they didn't and then felt even worse, blaming herself for her depression. In therapy Lisa began to explore how she could ask for what she needed from others, as well as express her angry feelings appropriately and to do more to take care of herself when she was feeling stressed.

While you may not always get what you want when you ask for it, you are more likely to get it if you are open about your needs and wishes than if you expect your partner, friend, or boss to gaze into a crystal ball and to guess what you want. And if other people cannot provide the support or affection you need at that time, you at least know where you stand and can do something about it.

Giving Yourself Attention

There is indeed another side of the coin to asking people for attention when you feel you need it, or to expecting them to know, as if by reading their crystal ball, just what you want whenever you want it. If you are not very good at giving yourself positive recognition, or at taking care of your own needs, you may become over-reliant on others, and have unrealistic expectations of relationships in which you are perpetually doomed to disappointment.

It is, therefore, important to become aware of the kinds of internal recognition and attention you give yourself. If you feel that you are a good enough person and you like yourself, you are likely to say to yourself, when you have made a special meal for friends, 'that looks good, I bet it will taste good, too'. If, on the other hand, you don't feel very good about yourself, you are more likely to say to yourself, 'I know my curry won't be very good, but of course, I'm a lousy cook anyway'. Even if your friends tell you how much they have enjoyed the meal, you may still prefer to believe that it wasn't a very good meal.

Sheila craved affection from others, but when her husband told her why he liked and loved her, she either didn't believe him or found it hard to hold on to what he said. In therapy, she gradually began to realise that unless she could learn to like herself she would continue to be like a sieve inside, in which good feedback got poured in, but simply ran right out again. Sheila needed to change her internal dialogue from one in which she continually criticised herself to one in which she came to like herself, warts and all and could see herself as a good enough person.

Beginnings in Childhood

The basis for the way in which we give, receive and respond to attention and recognition is usually formed in childhood. It is probably true to say that none of us ever 'sees things as they are', but only as we interpret them, according to our own unique past.

If, as a child, you were given lots of loving attention you will, in general, feel confident and competent about yourself. For example, if a colleague tells you that something you have done is stupid, you will either shrug it off if it is untrue, or be willing to consider what you can do about it if it is true. On the other hand, although your childhood may have been superficially happy and secure, you might have been discouraged in subtle ways from feeling good about yourself. When this happens, you tend to grow up with a lack of confidence in yourself and your abilities. You may also find that the cultural taboo about 'showing off' or appearing 'big-headed' or 'arrogant' makes it difficult for you to talk about your good qualities. If you were given lots of negative attention as a child you are very likely to have a negative view of yourself, and to lack confidence in your accomplishments and personal qualities. For example, you will, if told you look nice or have done something well, tend to ignore the comment or re-interpret it in some way so that it fits in with your negative image of yourself.

While it is preferable to have positive acknowledgement from others, you may, particularly if you received little positive attention as a child, tend to seek out negative recognition. For most people a total lack of recognition from others is unbearable, and we would probably prefer having a row with a partner to being totally ignored and treated as if we didn't exist. It is probably this need for recognition from others, as much as finances, concern for the children and so on, that keeps many people in unhappy relationships, as the alternative of being alone can seem to be so much worse.

Although most of us do give lots of affection and recognition to people we care about, we sometimes ration it as though we're afraid we might run out of affection or love. We tend to assume that people know, without us saying anything, the things we like and love about them. Or, if we are afraid to rock the boat by giving people any feedback that could be construed as criticism, we may, rather than dealing openly with differences, come to feel resentful, unhappy and dissatisfied.

Accepting the positive attention you get from others, giving it generously and being aware of your own qualities and talents provides a basis for good relationships. The kinds of attention and recognition you received as a child play an important part in the development of your adult personality. The purpose of the next three chapters is to take you back through childhood to help explain this development more fully.

Awareness Questionnaire

This questionnaire provides a quick checklist to help you begin to understand your recognition/attention profile (Exercise 1 in Chapter 11 will provide a more detailed opportunity to develop this profile). Put an X in the column that best fits you.

	Yes	No
1. I find it easy to tell people I'm close to: (a) that I care for them (b) what I value about them.		

	Yes	No
2. I find it easy to say positive things to people other than close friends or family.		
3. I find it easy to criticise people: (a) constructively (b) negatively.		
4. I tend to see the faults in: (a) other people I'm close to (b) other people generally (c) myself.		
5. I feel I don't get much positive attention from people.		
6. When I do, I find it hard to accept.		
7. When I receive constructive criticism, I always reject it, even if it might be valid.		
8. When I get unfair or unjust criticism, I find it hard to reject and get upset by it.		
9. I find it easy to ask people I'm close to for support, affection, etc.		
10. I find it easy to ask other people for support, help with work, etc.		
11. I find it easy to give myself good feedback and to take good care of myself.		

CHAPTER 3
The Child is Father of the Man

In my beginning is my end (T. S. Eliot)

Personality Development in Brief

As you grew from babyhood to adulthood, your personality developed three distinct parts. First, there is the part dealing primarily with your emotions, next the thinking, rational part and finally, the part which has opinions and values, takes care of people and sets limits on behaviour. The feeling part is called the *Child*, the thinking part the *Adult* and the ethical part the *Parent*. The use of capital initials for the words

Parent, Adult and Child indicate that they are being described in a rather different way from everyday usage. They are used within this model of behaviour to describe the various parts of the personality, rather than actual parents, adults or children.

Children, and some grown-ups, are not biological parents, but when they are behaving from the Parent part of their personality, and are being nurturing or controlling, they are using what is often seen as parenting behaviour. Neither are children adults, but when they are behaving from the Adult part of their personality, and are thinking and making decisions, they are using what is often seen as grown-up or adult behaviour. The serious child who has taken on a lot of responsibility at an early age is said to have 'an old head on young shoulders', implying that childhood isn't really a time for serious thought or behaviour. Conversely, as grown-ups, we are no longer children, but when we are behaving from the Child part of our personality, and are having fun or being creative, we are often being childlike (though not childish) in our behaviour, and getting close again to some of the pleasures and excitement we felt as children.

The *Child* Develops

The rest of this chapter will look in detail at the *Child*, or the part of your personality containing your creativity, intuition, sexuality and feelings, as well as the adaptations you learned to make, when young, to the demands of others.

When you were born, unless you were an identical twin, your mix of genes, instincts, physiological needs and so on was unique. Some of your instinctive behaviours, such as your sexuality, were present but not yet expressed, other than in the sensuality that is an integral part of early childhood. Although, from the moment of birth, this natural personality was being influenced and modified by the environment, you are, as a grown-up, the result of the interplay of nature and nurture.

As a young child, you did not have full information about what was happening around you, and thus could not make accurate or complete sense of it. You would have responded to situations emotionally rather than rationally. For example, a small child who keeps dropping his rattle on the floor and getting a cuddle from his mother as she picks it up will feel hurt and bewildered if he is suddenly smacked instead. He cannot know that, as he dropped his rattle again, the phone and the doorbell rang at the same time, and the milk also boiled over, leaving his mother angry and flustered with herself and her baby. The only information he had was that, for no apparent reason, he suddenly found himself being smacked instead of cuddled.

As children, we develop several aspects to the Child part of our personalities, and these go on influencing us as adults. A necessary part of growing up involves the adaptation of some of your natural or instinctive behaviours to the demands and expectations of the world around you, and the Child, it is said, has *natural*, *intuitive* and *adapted* characteristics. You can use these in ways that can enhance your personality and relationships with others. Alternatively, you may become involved in harmful behaviour of varying degrees of intensity, or you can over-adapt to the demands and expectations of others, and in doing so lose touch with your own genuine feelings and needs.

The Natural *Child*

A happy childhood includes a great deal of sensuality, fun, playfulness, creativity and spontaneous positive feelings. Very young children enjoy the sensuality of being breast fed, and cuddled, whereas older children continue to enjoy close physical contact with loving parents. Scrunching through crisp leaves, paddling through puddles, poking about the garden for insects, inventing stories or complicated games, drawing pictures, and so on all come quite naturally to small children. So does spontaneity of feeling. Children don't stop to think before they tell you they love you, or—temporarily at least—hate you, or before they give you a cuddle or sit on your knee, or before

they make a devastatingly accurate, though possibly hurtful, comment about your appearance or character.

The Intuitive *Child*

Small children also develop an intuitive part of their personality, by which they seem to know and understand things by hunch, rather than by having accurate information or knowledge. The child who hands her mother the car keys, even though she hasn't been told her mother's looking for them, or who gives her a cuddle and says 'don't worry' even though she apparently doesn't know her mother's concerned about her husband's late arrival home, is using intuitive thinking. Children have an uncanny ability to know whether people are being genuine or artificial with them. They may not know why things are the way they are, but they do learn how to respond to them in a way that seems to them, on the basis of the limited information they have at the time, most helpful for their own emotional survival.

The Adapted *Child*

When they are young, children also learn to respond to the demands and expectations of their parents. They learn how to use the potty, how to wash behind their ears, how to clean their teeth, and how to dress themselves. They also learn to eat with a knife and fork, rather than fingers, and to keep their food on their plates or in their mouths, rather than everywhere else. They learn to say 'please' and 'thank you', and to write to people thanking them for the Christmas presents they received. They find out what constitutes being a good boy or girl in their own particular family, how to be polite and well-behaved, and what feelings and behaviours are acceptable to their parents.

Much of children's early learning would have been through copying others. Small children playing 'mummies' and 'daddies' copy what they see and know about in their own

experience. In families where both parents work, or where the father shares the household chores, little girls may well be the ones who play at going out to work while their brothers stay home to mind the baby. In families where the mother is at home, 'mummy' will base her play on the way she has seen her own mother look after her, whilst 'daddy' may well be sent out to work, because that's what fathers do.

The *Child* in the Grown-up

So, if when you have grown up, the Child part of your personality hasn't been too restricted, you have available an emotional, intuitive, creative, sensual part of yourself. When you enjoy closeness with others, or success in work or leisure activities, or feel emotionally moved by music, or get a surge of excitement as you pot the black in snooker, you are involved in happy natural Child behaviours in which pleasurable feelings, such as excitement, joy or happiness are involved as well as, in some situations, feelings of closeness and intimacy. When you are creating something, such as a painting, building a model ship, or taking a photograph, you are using the creative, natural Child. Clearly, there are risks in some

activities, and this can be part of the excitement, but when the Child is being used well, you are aware of the risks, minimise them as much as you can, and behave responsibly in the way you handle them. You will also usually need to use Adult information and knowledge in order to achieve your ends, but the fun, the achievement and the creative ideas stem from the Child.

It is useful to be able to use your adapted Child to deal with some everyday behaviours automatically, without, in a sense, having to think about them. Small children need teaching, and then reminding, to wash their necks, but you can remember that when you get up, you need to wash, shave and so on. When you meet a neighbour or a colleague, or buy a ticket to go on a train journey, you know, without having to think about it, the conventions for greetings, and for polite ways of asking for information. These helpful adaptations 'oil the wheels' of daily living and help you to get along easily with others, as well as making you easier to live with and more pleasant to have around!

The *Child* can be Destructive, Too

Unfortunately, the Child is often boxed in, pushed or pummelled until it is a shadow of its former self. Or it may be left so much to its own devices in early childhood that it has no ability to know the difference between real enjoyment and hysterical or destructive fun, or how to differentiate between a spontaneity that also takes account of others' feelings and one that is purely self-centred.

Philip is in his forties and, to colleagues and friends, he appears as a successful and well-to-do businessman. But internally Philip feels very different. When things go wrong, he feels intense hurt and upset to a degree which is out of all proportion to the event and describes himself as feeling very childlike. We have only just begun to explore the roots of his childlike feelings, but they appear to stem from a childhood in which he felt stifled by an over-protective mother and neglected by a workaholic and often absent father. Neither parent set appropriate behavioural boundaries and Philip has spent much of his life getting into scrapes, first as a child and then in adult work and personal relationships. He is aware that he is seeking approval and affection, yet continues to find himself in situations where he doesn't get positive attention, thus repeating the childhood pattern in which he failed to get the kind of love he needed. Philip is very committed to change and, as he is beginning to make more sense of his current behaviour, he is trying out new and more effective ways of dealing with situations in which he feels unreasonable hurt. He is beginning to find that if he can communicate more clearly from the grown-up part of his personality, he is getting better results and that more open relationships are developing.

Sometimes, people use the natural Child in a destructive or over-impulsive way: they may drink heavily at a party, and then take risks as they drive home. Getting involved in hurtful, destructive personal relationships, physical violence or drug misuse are all examples of the destructive Child. Sometimes, the lives of famous and creative people reflect this duality: they may produce work that gives much pleasure to their public and lead glamourous and exciting lives. But their creativity can often go hand-in-hand with relationship or personality difficulties, or with alcohol or drug abuse.

Sometimes, there is only a thin line between the spontaneous Child and one that is destructively impulsive, and 'living for kicks'. We live in a culture in which change and excitement is encouraged and this can result in a sort of frenetic desire for more and more stimulation, with bigger and better surges of adrenalin. It seems that we have to balance the needs we have for excitement with the ability to be at peace with ourselves, both physically and emotionally.

For some people, though, the adapted Child is used negatively. If you do not have much fun or excitement in your life or you have, in the name of 'good sense' and 'being mature' damped down your very important Child needs, you might feel that you would like to find ways of rediscovering or developing these.

The negative adapted Child is also in evidence if you frequently feel anxious, 'put down', depressed, or guilty, or if you spend all your time pleasing others. You may do so because you learnt, early in childhood, to become too compliant and too concerned to meet others' expectations of you. Alternatively, you may spend a lot of your time feeling angry or frustrated, or complaining that everyone else is a fool. If this is the case, you have probably learnt, as a child, that the only safe feelings to express are angry ones. Or you may believe that the only way to get people to do what you want is to be angry, even though your behaviour may mean that you are not greatly liked, or that you find yourself isolated.

The Feeling *Child*

Being able to respond to situations with feelings as well as thoughts and opinions is an essential part of being fully grown up. We all need to keep a strong and happy Child as an essential part of our personality, as well as being able to appreciate the very real difference between mature use of the Child in a grown-up, and childish behaviour which is immature, inappropriate and possibly harmful. Jumping over boulders, splashing in the sea, dancing at a party are Child behaviours, whereas throwing tantrums, or driving dangerously are childish behaviours.

In order to understand this fully, you need to think back to your own childhood, and to consider what kinds of behaviour, feelings, and attitudes you were encouraged to develop and what, if any, were frowned upon. Clearly, parents need to set some limits on their children's behaviour, but there are families where children are overly encouraged to be good, to always be clean and tidy, and so on. Such children may also be encouraged to further their 'goodness' by taking care of their parents, becoming sensitive to mummy's need for quiet because of her frequent migraines, or by being seen, but not heard, so that daddy can have some peace. When such children are, in their parents' eyes, naughty, the disapproval they get, and the distress they cause their parents, can make them so unhappy that they quickly learn to take up their good behaviour again.

As adults, such people are over-compliant, apologising to you before they have done anything to upset you, going beyond the call of duty in whatever they do, and taking so much care of you that you may develop what C. S. Lewis called the 'hunted look'[1] of those who are being done good to.

When adults, children with this kind of background are also likely to find that their creative, fun-loving Child has become starved, repressed and unhappy—and this is not likely to go away. What it may do is to set up a protest in the form of feelings of guilt, resentment and so on, or illnesses such as anxiety states, depression, or psychosomatic complaints.

I am not, for one moment, suggesting that everyone flings such concepts as duty or care and concern for others to the winds. What I am suggesting is that you need to be in tune with both your own and others' needs and desires, and to balance your giving to others with an ability both to give to yourself and to receive from others.

In some families, where the parents are disadvantaged in various ways, where they have learnt to repress their loving feelings, or where the child rebels against being good, children may grow up being angry, seeing themselves as victims, and seeing injustices and slights at every turn. If you feel anger as an automatic, rather than a considered, response to situations, then you are likely to have learnt that this is the only way to survive. This constant anger can also result in psychosomatic and stress-related illnesses, in a high level of frustration, in constant battles with other people, and in difficulties in forming close relationships.

Again, I am not saying that anger is never useful. Anger about poverty, unemployment, damage to the environment and so on can be used, in conjunction with the thinking Adult, to act to change things. Indeed, learning to express anger constructively can sometimes be an important part of the counselling process, as all too often, anger turns inwards and becomes depression. But, as with the compliant person, what I am suggesting is the importance of being in tune with your whole self, and of taking good care of yourself and others by ensuring that if you feel anger it is positive and appropriate rather than destructive.

When I first met Katie, she was depressed and unhappy and couldn't say anything positive about herself at all. I soon learnt that Katie had been sexually abused as a child, but had never spoken about it to anyone. She felt anger, not only against the abusers, but also against her mother, whom she felt should have protected her. Over the years, this unexpressed anger had turned itself into depression, so that Katie had come to believe that she was responsible for the abuse. She felt bad about herself and couldn't think of anything about herself that was likeable. Gradually, during counselling, she allowed her anger to surface and to be experienced. As a result, she became a much happier person, and was able to develop a closer relationship with her mother after many years of emotional distance.

The Value of the *Child*

The Child is a very essential part of your personality. It is the source of fun, and of happy, joyful, sexual, creative feelings and behaviour. If your Child is overly-restricted or destructive, you may find that your life is all work and no play, or that you behave in ways that are harmful to yourself and others. With a positive and happy Child you have time for work and play, the potential for developing close, loving relationships, and the ability to deal constructively with emotional and other crises if they occur. If you use your Child well, it usually means that you are happier, more energetic and more—not less—loving to the people about whom you care.

It should be noted that the Child can only function really effectively if it is integrated into the total personality. Without the thinking ability of the Adult and the nurturing and limit-setting role of the Parent, our personality would be overwhelmed by feelings and we would probably feel chaotic, confused and out of control. At times of stress, illness or unhappiness, we tend to retreat into the Child, and to feel vulnerable and as if we are actually back at a much younger age.

When I have to go to work on dark, miserable mornings in the winter my Child can sometimes feel very resentful, preferring to be at home. I need all the force of my Adult and some firm talking from my Parent to remind me that, not only do I need to earn my living, but once I'm on my way, I usually enjoy my work. Equally, when I am using my Child creativity in writing a story for my nieces, or taking a photograph, I also need Adult information and knowledge in order to get the outcome I want. When I am tired, my Parent needs to come to my assistance, so that I can decide how best to relax. I might choose an early night, a relaxing sauna or massage, music or time spent with close friends.

Chapter 4 takes the development of personality further by looking at the Adult, which is the next step in the emotional growth of young children.

Recognising the *Child*

Although Exercise 2 in Chapter 11 gives you a further opportunity to explore the Child part of your own personality, this checklist can give you a chance to begin to recognise Child behaviours and feelings. It lists some everyday behaviours—you need to decide which of the aspects of the Child it is likely to be describing: positive natural Child (+NC); negative natural Child (–NC); the intuitive Child (IC); positive adapted Child (+AC); negative adapted Child (–AC). As we are all different, there won't necessarily be one right answer, but the purpose of the checklist is to give you practice at recognising the various elements of the Child.

Put +NC, etc. (as appropriate) in the right-hand column.

1. Giving a friend a hug.
2. Saying 'please' and 'thank you'.
3. Getting angry when waiting in a traffic jam.

4. Feeling excited about a work promotion.
5. Enjoying the sun and the sea on holiday.
6. Feeling stupid when you forget to post some letters.
7. Getting so angry at a meeting you storm out.
8. Checking out a hunch by ringing a friend to see if he is OK.
9. Holding the door open for someone to go in front of you.
10. Pulling strings at work to get your own way about a new project.
11. Narrowly avoiding an accident.
12. Buying some new clothes.
13. Eating a bar of chocolate.
14. Making up a story for a child.
15. Feeling sad when your cat dies.

CHAPTER 4
Think for Yourself

Come, live in Now and occupy it well (Robert Graves)

As a grown-up, you need the ability to think clearly, whether you are choosing new wallpaper, doing car repairs, caring for a sick child or making business transactions. You also have to make decisions, both large and small, every day of your life, whether you are deciding about a new job, what to have for lunch, or how long to allow for a journey.

You also have to find ways of reconciling the conflicts between what you feel you want to do (sitting in the sun, having a cream-cake) and what you feel you ought to do (cleaning the car, saving for a rainy day) or have to do (going to work, doing a duty visit to someone).

This thinking, decision-making, mediating part of your personality is called the *Adult*. It did not suddenly emerge as a nicely packaged extra present when you reached the age of

majority, but started developing in early childhood as you began to make connections between cause and effect, to ask questions, to find things out for yourself and to think logically.

The Developing *Adult*

As children learn to speak, they also begin to ask a lot of questions. Why must I eat my cabbage up? How high is the sky? Where do babies come from? What's for tea, I'm starving? When is Christmas ... is it soon?

They are also concerned with finding out how to do things, and how things work, as well as finding out how to behave in order to please their parents. They learn how to tie their laces and button up their shirts or blouses. When their sandcastles collapse, they may want to find out why, so that they can build them differently. They learn not to interrupt when dad is watching his favourite football team on television, or to keep quiet if mum is sounding cross.

They also begin to make decisions for themselves—about what to wear, how to spend their pocket money, what games to play, what television programme to watch or who is going to be their favourite friend. Their parents would probably also give them choices—about whether to have fish-fingers or spaghetti for tea, or whether to go swimming or to play in the park.

The Influence of Parents

When you are grown up, your ability to use your Adult depends, to a great extent, on what happened to you as a child. Parents who answer their children's questions, encouraging them to find out how to do things for themselves, and allowing them to make decisions and to develop their interests—be it in dinosaurs, insects or train spotting—are likely to find that their children grow up well able to think clearly for themselves.

Parents are obviously not perfect and they all, at times, find that their own needs interfere with their parenting. They

get tired, or irritable or have problems of their own to cope with
and they may not always want to answer interminable questions
or play yet another game of snakes and ladders. Most children
are told, at some time, to 'go and play' or 'see if there's anything to watch on television'. Indeed, part of the process of
growing up is discovering that other people have needs, too. As
long as there is a basic love and security, most children can
cope well with their parents' imperfections and still develop a
good, clear Adult which they then have available, as grown-
ups, for their own use.

Sometimes parents can over-protect their children, by
doing things for them, rather than encouraging them to do
things for themselves. Instead of letting their children dress
themselves, they hurry them along by dressing them. If their
children want to climb trees, or ride a bike, or go camping, they
tell them it's dangerous, or dirty, or wet or cold. If their children
want to find out how to do things for themselves, they discourage this by such comments as 'give it to me, I'll do it for you'.

Alternatively, parents may be so pre-occupied with their
own concerns and needs that they fail to give their children any
clear structure from which to develop a strong Adult. When
their children ask questions they say 'don't bother me now, I'm
busy'. When they seek help with a jigsaw or show off a drawing they've done, their needs and achievements are greeted
with indifference, criticism or rejection.

The *Adult* in Adults

If, as a child, you lived in such an over-protective, indifferent or rejecting family, you may find that you have difficulty
now in using your Adult. You are likely to be indecisive, relying on other people to help you to make decisions. You may
tend to confuse feelings with thinking, relying on your Child
emotions or Parent opinions when you really need Adult thinking in order to make decisions and to solve problems.

When the Adult is being used well and effectively, it acts
as a mediator. If you have a problem in which you feel you are

'going round in circles', it may well be that you are having an internal conflict between what you want to do and what you feel you ought to do. This can be about quite simple things, like deciding whether to take a day's leave if you only have a slight cold. Or it can be about complex situations, such as a major job or home change. You may, for example, feel that you want to take the new job you've been offered, but that you ought to turn it down, as it means changes in your children's schooling and moving away from your elderly parents.

When this happens, the Child and Parent are in a sort of internal quarrel with each other, with the Child nudging you to do what you want, and the Parent urging you to do your duty. It is important not to ignore feelings as, if you do, they have a way of sabotaging or undermining decisions you have made. It is equally important not to ignore ethical issues and responsibilities you may have taken on. Whilst there may not be an ideal solution, thinking things through with the Adult, rather than working entirely on feelings or opinions can help you examine all the options available to you, to sort out facts from Child feelings and Parent opinions, and to find the best (not always the most obvious) solution.

When Ken first came to see me, he was confused about whether or not to stay in a relationship with a girlfriend who was unwilling to make the total commitment of marriage. His Parent argued that he should give her up, whilst his Child said he wanted to stay in the relationship, despite some unhappy aspects. By using the Adult in counselling, he faced up to the fact that he couldn't make her change. But he decided that he would stay in the relationship and find some more effective ways of handling the aspects that made him unhappy. He had given up a good deal of his previously independent lifestyle and decided that he would reclaim some of this, so that the bits of his life which had to be separate from his girlfriend would be more rewarding.

Imagine that a friend rings up, wanting you see you immediately about an urgent problem. You may feel you ought to see her, as she is clearly worried, but you may also feel that, after a hard day's work, you just want to go home and relax. If you follow your Parent values only, you might see her immediately, and not be as helpful as you would normally be, because you are feeling tired, and, possibly, a bit resentful. If you follow your Child needs only, your relaxed evening might well be marred by a feeling that you haven't lived up to your own standards of caring for others. If you use your Adult, you could suggest that your friend comes to see you later in the evening, after you have relaxed and had a meal.

Because you use your Adult for thinking and decision-making, it is an essential part of your personality. It is also needed to act in conjunction with the positive elements of your Child and Parent. When you decide where to go on holiday, your Child decides (I want sun, sea, and sand or I want lots to see and do) in conjunction with the Adult (what can I afford and when can I go?), what it wants and where to go. When you decide to take a day off work with a heavy cold, your Parent decides (I'm feeling really miserable and just want a day in bed), in conjunction with the Adult (I wouldn't be able to do anything useful, feeling like this), that this is the best way to take care of your health and to avoid spreading your cold to others.

The Cost of Ignoring the *Adult*

If you fail to use your Adult in conjunction with your Child or Parent, you will find that you tend to use these parts of your personality in ways that are negative or unhelpful. Your Adult helps the Child to differentiate between what is real fun and what is dangerous, between being polite and being overly compliant and a doormat, or between genuine, appropriate emotional responses to situations and archaic, out-of-date ones. It also helps the Parent to differentiate between genuine care and being over-nurturing and between the setting of realistic limits or punitive, critical ones. Although a good and effective Adult is essential, it is also important to recognise the value and importance of each part of the personality. No one part is better than another—we each develop a unique blend of Parent, Adult, Child feelings and behaviour. It is when we get into communication tangles, or work or personal difficulties that we might feel that there is a need to change some aspects of our attitudes or behaviour.

An effective Adult is essential to emotional health and maturity. You cannot think clearly or make good decisions without it. If there is no Adult available to work with the positive elements of your Child and Parent, they too, tend to be impoverished.

Thinking and feeling alone do not make a whole person as the Parent—the subject of Chapter 5—is needed to complete the picture.

Putting the *Adult* in Charge

Exercise 3 in Chapter 11 provides an opportunity for you to look at the way in which the Adult can be used for problem solving, while this short questionnaire can get you thinking about how well you deal with crises. At times of crisis, it can sometimes be difficult to put the Adult in charge. You can test out your Adult reactions by looking at the following situations. Be aware of your Child reactions (fear, excitement, etc.), but focus mainly on what your Adult reactions and behaviour might be.

1. You wake up and think you can hear burglars in the house.
2. You find you have unexpectedly won or inherited £5,000.
3. You find you have unexpectedly won or inherited £50,000.
4. You have been asked to do a parachute jump for charity.
5. You have arrived at an important function completely over-dressed in full evening suit or dress.
6. You are faced with someone who has cut a hand badly and is still bleeding—all over your new carpet.
7. You have made a major mistake at work.
8. You have been rejected for a job you very much wanted.
9. You have had a blazing row with a lover/partner/friend.
10. You have forgotten you invited friends for dinner and they are standing on the doorstep just as you have settled down for the evening.

CHAPTER 5

Parents are People, Too

Children begin by loving their parents; after a time
they judge them; rarely, if ever, do they forgive them
(Oscar Wilde)

The *Parent* part of your personality acts very much as a real parent, by being nurturing and setting limits on behaviour. It also contains values, beliefs, opinions and prejudices, and thus acts as the moral or ethical part of your personality. You first develop your own Parent within your family, taking on, though sometimes adapting, the parenting behaviours, values and attitudes you meet there, and using them, in your turn, as the nurturing, controlling or ethical part of your personality.

The *Parent* Develops

Your parents are normally your first model of what parenting is all about. They would have had their own particular way of taking care of your physical and emotional needs. They would also have passed on their expectations of you, as well as their beliefs, values and attitudes, and their views about how you should fit in to the culture and society in which you live. They would have done this by example (their behaviour and attitudes acting as a model for you to follow); by attributing certain characteristics to you (Mary's going to be a doctor, just like her father) or, less strongly, by suggestion (it would be nice if Johnny became a doctor).

Being a parent is a complex, time-consuming and lengthy business. Unlike most other animals, human babies remain dependent for a very long time. Although the age of majority is now eighteen, and young people are physically capable of

45

creating families of their own well before that age, they are still not emotionally fully mature and are rarely financially independent by then. Thus parents have to meet their children's changing physical and emotional needs from birth, through adolescence and into young adulthood. To understand how your Parent develops, and what part it plays in your personality, you need to understand your parents, and the many different tasks of parenting in your culture.

Being a Parent

Parents have to respond to their children's changing physical needs. They provide milk for tiny babies, and persuasion for older children as they try to convince them that, for example, fresh fruit and vegetables are better for them than burgers and chips. They bathe grazed knees, and wash dirty clothes, whether these are from a fall in the playground or, later, from playing football on a muddy field.

Parents also take care of their children's emotional needs. They are a source of security, listening to their children as they talk about their successes and worries at school, the death of a pet or their hopes, and sometimes fears, for the future. They give advice as small children cry about being bullied at school or, later, as older children sob about a broken heart.

Parents also set limits on their children's impulsive and self-centred behaviour. They teach them to share their toys, to say 'please' and 'thank you' or to tidy their rooms. They teach them that they can't have all the sweets they want, and that having a temper tantrum won't work, that hitting their friends is not the way to solve arguments, or that they can't have all the attention they want whenever they want it. Parents are people, too, and they need to balance their children's needs with their own.

Parents also pass on to their children beliefs, opinions, values and prejudices. Children who are taught that 'we're all the same under the skin' probably grow up free from racial prejudice, whereas children who are told that 'you can't trust foreigners, black people, or Jews' are liable to grow up with racist and bigoted views. Children who are taught to appreciate that the world is still a place of beauty and delight may develop a concern for other people and the environment, whereas children who are told that the world is an ugly or dangerous place may become indifferent to their surroundings or suspicious of other people.

Parents also pass on their expectations and wishes for their children. They may say things such as 'do as well as you can and enjoy what you do' or 'girls don't need education, they'll get married' or 'we expect you to do better than us' or 'we want you to be happy'. Sometimes, the expectation isn't spelt out in words, but in the way parents respond to their children. The father who, in the swimming pool, responds to his son's successful shout of 'I've swum a length' with 'now do it again, backstroke' may well be teaching his son that whatever he does isn't good enough, but has to be done differently or better. The father who responds with a hug and 'that's great' will be teaching his son that he is good enough and giving him confidence.

The *Parent* as a Product of the Family

As you grew up you would have learnt, from the model of parenting you had in your own home, how to take care of people and how to set limits on behaviour. You might also have misinterpreted or re-interpreted some of the things your parents said or did, or their expectations of you, making up, in a sense, your own version of events. You might also, as you experienced a wider range of influences, have rebelled against some of these parental expectations, and updated or modified some of your views. Nevertheless, whatever the changes and development in your Parent as you have grown up, you are still likely to be very much the product of your own particular family and culture. Your Parent, like your Child and your Adult, is primarily formed and influenced by the experiences you had when you were young.

You can see the Parent developing quite clearly in young children. Although they are too young to take on the real task of

parenting, they can, and do, show care and concern for people—for a friend who falls down in the playground, a parent
who is upset, or a pet who is ill or hurt. They can also be very
bossy and controlling in their games, especially to younger or
smaller children. They also have beliefs, opinions and values:
that Father Christmas is real, that A's ice-cream is better than
B's, or that people shouldn't fight and kill each other.

Like the Child, the Parent can either enhance your personality and your life, or it can be repressive and destructive. As
with the Child, the Parent needs to be monitored through the
Adult if it is to be well and effectively used. The Child is very
much concerned with wants, fun, creativity and spontaneity,
whereas the Parent is concerned with oughts and shoulds, values, opinions, duty and responsibility. Also like the Child, the
Parent has various aspects. It can be either positively or negatively *nurturing* or *controlling*.

The Nurturing *Parent*

When the nurturing Parent is used positively, you can be
loving and caring in your relationships. When people need help,
you can give the support, advice, time, or information that they

need in a way that still allows them to find their own way through the problem, and doesn't smother them with help. You also take care not to lose sight of your own needs for relaxation, and so on. Visiting a friend who is ill, listening carefully while a colleague talks about a work or domestic problem, taking your partner a cup of early morning tea, are examples of Parent care for others. Having an early night when you are tired, deciding that some jobs can be left until tomorrow, relaxing with friends or with music, or through yoga, are all examples of Parent care of yourself.

The Over-nurturing *Parent*

It can sometimes be difficult to get a reasonable balance between care of yourself and care of others. If you are looking after young children, or an elderly or disabled relative, holding down a stressful job, coping with unemployment or poverty, you may find that time for yourself gets swallowed up by the needs of others, the business of earning a living, or just surviving from one week to the next. You may also have a built-in sense of guilt which operates, both to keep you doing your duty at all costs, and to spoil any attempts you may occasionally make to take some time for yourself.

Sometimes, people only feel good about themselves if they are rushing around, being busy and useful, and doing things for other people. If you have to do a lot of caring for others, you may find you have a tendency to be over-helpful. If people seem to think you have nothing better to do than to give them lifts or do bits of shopping for them, or bail them out of yet another financial crisis, or if you always seem to be offering help, even if you haven't been asked for it, you may be using your Parent in a way that is smothering for other people and discourages them from finding their own solutions to problems.

One of my friends provides a salutory and amusing example of the problems of being over-helpful. She once found a dog wandering around a building site and assumed it to be lost. She took it home and spent several frustrating hours trying to find its owners. Eventually, she took it to the police station, where it was put into the dog pound. Next day, she discovered that the dog's owner was a pensioner who had been working on the building site and had taken his dog to work with him for company. Having discovered that his dog was missing, he had gone to the police and had to pay ten pounds to get him back. As far as the dog was concerned, the final insult must have been when he found himself left at home next day, in case he wandered off again.

Doing a lot for others, and ignoring your own needs, whether it stems from your need to be helpful all the time, or from having to care for people who are very dependent, can be physically and emotionally tiring. Failing to set limits on your helpful, nurturing qualities may mean that, as you get more and more exhausted from being permanently helpful, you come to feel angry, resentful or frustrated with the demands you feel are being made on you. If you don't give time to looking after yourself, you may well find that you begin to suffer from stress of various kinds. A nagging resentment may turn into feelings of depression, a cold which is ignored may become worse, becoming over-tired may result in an accident.

It can be all too easy to lose sight of your own needs to recharge and relax, but unless you do this, your care and concern for others will, eventually, also be negatively affected. It is my belief that the quality of our care for others is closely bound up with our ability to care for ourselves. If you do not give time and energy to your own needs, you will find it difficult to go on giving loving, genuine care to others without becoming tired, stressed, resentful and, possibly, ill yourself.

I have found, since I became interested in the management of stress, that while stressful situations haven't magically disappeared, giving time to myself is a very constructive way of dealing with them. I have developed a range of ways of taking care of my own needs when under pressure at work or home and I find that, rather than having less time and energy, I seem to have more. What some people might see as being selfish or giving into myself acts in fact as a way of recharging my energy.

The Controlling *Parent*

When the controlling Parent is used well and positively, you are able to be assertive (as opposed to aggressive) when involved in aspects of setting limits—giving instructions, chairing a meeting, complaining about faulty goods, getting children to take on some of the household chores. You give clear information and, where possible, positive feedback when, for instance, a piece of work has been done well. You can also be protective to people who are at risk—shouting 'stop' to a child who is about to touch a hot stove is, for example, a good use of control. You can also set positive limits on yourself—saying 'no' to the excessive demands of work, family or friends; taking a break when you are tired; finding time, if you have a busy job, to relax; ensuring, if you have children, that you get some time to yourself.

You may find you use your controlling Parent in a less positive way. You may feel uncomfortable if you are not the person who is in control, believing you can't trust colleagues enough to delegate work to them, even though you then become exhausted. You may refuse help in the home, while feeling hard done by, or be dominating and organising in your friendships, yet feel resentful that no one else takes on any responsibility for organising theatre tickets, or trips. Or you may be over critical, always on the lookout for the flaws in people and situations—and making sure you find them.

Even if a friendship, or a new job, or a different house, begin well you soon find fault and feel yourself to be disappointed or let down. You may be even more critical of yourself, having a running internal dialogue in which you castigate yourself for all your faults, real or imagined, past, present and sometimes future. Your dialogue is full of things you ought or should have done or said, and you will back it up with a good measure of guilty or anxious feelings.

When I first met Alan, he was depressed and saw himself as being no good. It soon became clear that he spent much of his time listening to a very critical internal Parent. Although I could see that he was an interesting, intelligent person he saw himself as boring and a failure. As a result, he behaved in ways that comfortably reinforced his internal dialogue. Gradually, he began to turn down the volume on his negative internal dialogue and to see himself in a more positive light.

If you tend to use your Parent in an unhelpful way, you may well have had some unhappy and traumatic experiences in childhood which still continue to influence and, perhaps, to haunt you. Or you may have experienced subtle, but none the less unhelpful, pressures and expectations which also continue to take their toll in terms of negative attitudes and behaviours, often in relation to feelings about yourself not being good enough.

Suzanne came to see me because she was having panic attacks. We found that she tended to have unrealistically high expectations of herself and that she wanted to be in control of any situation in which she found herself. As long as she was working and in control of the family or the office, she could keep the anxiety at bay, but when she had a chance to relax and enjoy herself, panic tended to surface. Suzanne was able to use simple relaxation and breathing exercises to help her; she was also able to see how her early childhood had influenced her. At one point in her childhood her father had left home and the family had experienced real poverty. As a result, Suzanne had an internal Parent that approved of working hard, but disapproved of fun or enjoyment in case it led to disaster. Seeing the difference between the reality of the past (poverty and stress) and the reality of the present (a successful business and happy marriage) also helped Suzanne to manage her feelings of panic more appropriately.

You need a good and effective Parent so that you can make ethical and moral decisions, look after people when necessary, and set appropriate limits on others' behaviour. Your Parent is also used to help you look after yourself, by co-operating with the Child. It can help to set limits on the destructive elements in the Child, as well as taking care of the Child part of yourself when it is tired, unhappy or stressed. So your Parent needs to be an open, flexible part of your personality, which can, in conjunction with the Adult, think about changing attitudes and values, and adapt and respond appropriately.

Recognising the *Parent*

There is an opportunity to examine the influence of your
Parent on you in Exercise 4 in Chapter 11. This questionnaire
gives you a chance to begin to identify your own Parent
characteristics. Make a list of:

1. The *oughts* and *shoulds* by which you live your life, e.g. I
    should always wash up before I go to bed.
2. The ways in which you nurture or take care of other peo-
    ple, e.g. I really listen to people when they are unhappy or
    confused.
3. The ways in which you take care of yourself, e.g. I make
    sure I get some time to relax every day.
4. Your strategies for setting limits on others, e.g. I shout at
    people who demand too much of me.
5. Your strategies for setting limits on yourself, e.g. I give
    myself a really hard time if I don't meet my own
    standards.

CHAPTER 6
The Complete Person

Don't be afraid of yourself, live your individuality to the full (Dag Hammarskjöld)

The Integrated *Adult*

So far, each of the basic elements that make up adult personality have been examined separately. In order to get on effectively with everyday living, you need to be able to use the Parent, Adult and Child in an integrated way. This means using your Adult to monitor the constructive use of Child and Parent, that is, to integrate your feelings with your thinking skills, your nurturing ability and your values about how to live. For each of us, the way this integration takes place will depend on the way our personality develops. And for each of us, it will be incomplete, as there will always be times when, usually under stress, we flip into the unintegrated parts of the personality.

When I am working in a therapy session, I need, for example, to have my Adult available so that I can think clearly about what is happening and what I am saying and why. I need my Parent in order to set boundaries on time, or to give encouragement and support as clients struggle with changing behaviour, or to set constructive controls if their behaviour seems to be destructive. Finally, I need my Child's intuition and liking for my clients if I am to be emotionally open to them.

Personality isn't a Static Thing

As you grow from babyhood to adulthood, each part of your personality changes and develops, depending on what happens to you and on how you use your experience. Once you are grown up, although there may well be some changes and developments in the way you use your Parent, Adult and Child, your personality and behaviour is normally fairly consistent. It would be difficult for you, and for the people around you if you put on a new personality each day in the same way as you put on a change of clothes. You also tend to reinforce your own particular type of personality by choosing a lifestyle that fits in with it. For example, people who choose jobs in the caring professions, or involving authority tend to have a strong Parent, people who choose jobs such as computing, accountancy, science or the law tend to have a strong Adult; and people who choose the world of the arts, or the media tend to have a strong Child.

Although your basic personality is formed, you may find that, at different stages in your adult life, one part of your personality has to come to the fore even if this is temporarily at the expense of other parts. If you are studying hard for exams, your Adult is working overtime. When you are the parent of a small child, you need to use your Parent very fully. If a relationship ends, your Child feels sadness and loss.

Whilst all three parts of your personality are essential and important, their positive use depends on your ability to move flexibly and appropriately from one part to another, depending on the situation. If your child or partner has a cold, she doesn't want an Adult lecture on viruses or bacteria, but needs Parent

nurturing. If you are thinking about buying a new family car, and are on a fairly tight budget, your Child fantasies about an expensive, fast sports car are probably best left as fantasies, while your Adult decides on the best type of car for your pocket and lifestyle. If you are at a party or a dance, you may find you enjoy it less if you have left your Child at home, and instead spend your time talking about the latest sales figures and projections to all who cross your path.

In a normal day, you are likely to move between Parent, Adult and Child dozens of times, often very rapidly. The following might, for example, go on inside your head when you wake up on a dark, cold winter morning. It may only take a few seconds, but requires a shift from Child, through Parent to Adult.

'I don't like the look of the day—think I'll stay here and keep warm' (Child).

'Come on, now, you ought to get up—you've got a lot to do' (Parent).

'I think I can stretch to another five minutes in bed, and still catch the bus—I hate this cold weather, but work calls' (Adult).

Sometimes, you use all the parts of your personality simultaneously. If you are first on the scene at an accident, your Parent provides comfort and concern, your Adult decides how best to deal with it, whilst your Child may feel anxious about doing the right things, and upset about what has happened.

As long as you can shift flexibly and appropriately between your Parent, Adult and Child, you probably feel happy with yourself as you are, even though it may well be appropriate for you to use, say, Adult, a good deal more than your Parent or Child because of your job or lifestyle. Your Parent, Adult and Child usually co-operate with each other, and although they are very unlikely to be used entirely equally, they are in a good balance with each other.

Problems in Personality Development

Although we all vary enormously in the ways in which we use our personality, you can begin to appreciate fully the importance of each part if you imagine what it would be like to have one or more parts either missing or, more commonly, very much underused. If your Adult was missing, you would be confused in your behaviour, as you went round in circles between your *wants* and what you *ought* to do. If your Parent was missing, you would have little, if any, sense of right or wrong, and be quite unable to take care of yourself or others, or to set boundaries around your own or others' behaviour. If your Child was missing, you would be like Jack, who was (because life was all work and no play) a dull boy. You would be serious, thoughtful and dutiful, but no fun.

Many of the people I see in therapy and workshops are spending much of their time as carers, either in their home or in their work in the helping professions. When they learn about the concept of the fun-loving, creative, natural Child there is, for many of them, a real sense of discovery, as though they have found the missing bit of themselves. Much of my time is spent encouraging people to reclaim their Child creativity and fun, without losing their very real sense of concern for others.

Although people rarely have parts of the personality completely missing, some very much over-use one part at the expense of the other two. If you found yourself operating almost entirely from one part of the personality, life would be liable to be difficult. If you were entirely Child, you would be like a child in a grown-up body: infantile, chaotic, impulsive, loving and affectionate, but with no real ability to think or make decisions for yourself. If you were entirely Adult, you would be rather like a robot, or a computer, churning out facts and figures but incapable of fun, closeness or nurturing. If you were entirely Parent, you would be a sort of permanent earth mother (or father), always taking care of (and perhaps trying to control) others but incapable of having fun or thinking clearly.

Jean is an example of someone who sees herself as operating very much from one part of her personality, rather than from an integration of Parent, Adult and Child. Jean described herself, when I first met her, as a little girl, despite the fact that she was married and a mother. As a child, Jean had a very critical mother and she feels that she was never really allowed to develop any independent ideas or thoughts of her own. Jean sees herself as over-using her adapted Child and controlling Parent in a negative way, and very much under-using the other parts of her personality. She feels she has very little Adult available for use, and described herself, when we first met, as being about eight emotionally. As Jean begins to think for herself and to make decisions, she is developing an effective Adult part of her personality, and now sees herself as being an adolescent, but still with several years' growing up to do.

Getting a good balance between the Parent, Adult and Child does not mean being dull, or ordinary, or having a life which lacks excitement. It does mean finding your own personal way of being a 'whole' person, and of living out your individuality. That is, having a sense of concern for self, others and the world around you, thinking clearly, and having a zest for life. This balance is expressed in liking yourself, in an ability to sustain loving relationships, and in enjoying life, though remaining aware of the many serious problems faced by people in today's world.

Parent/Adult/Child Checklist

Chapter 11 does not give a specific exercise in relation to the integrated personality. All the ideas and exercises in this book are based on the belief that it is possible, through understanding and (if necessary) change, to develop a more integrated personality. This checklist gives you a chance to reflect on some of the ideas so far. Consider the situations below, and in the first column put your initial reaction. It may come very strongly from one particular part of your personality, or there may be a mixture. In the second column, put down any alternative reactions that might have been better for you. Use +NP, −NP, +CP, −CP, +NC, −NC, +AC, −AC to indicate positive and negative use of the nurturing and controlling Parent, and natural and adapted Child. Use A for an Adult response.

	1	2
1. You have failed to keep an important work deadline.		
2. Someone you love has said something critical to you.		
3. Someone unimportant to you has said something critical.		
4. You have too many demands on your time.		
5. On the beach your neighbour turns on a loud radio.		
6. Someone you like tells you you're wonderful.		
7. Someone you don't like tells you you're wonderful.		
8. You have the chance of a weekend abroad, but also a heavy work schedule or problems of childminding.		
9. A parent living alone some way away is ill at home.		
10. You've been offered a new job, but it means moving home.		
11. You're given a trip in a hot-air balloon as a present.		
12. You've had a bonus and want a new kitchen and exotic holiday, but can't afford both.		
13. You've been made redundant with a generous lump sum.		
14. Someone offers to read your fortune in your hand.		
15. A neighbour calls for a chat when you are very busy.		
16. The central heating breaks down in a cold spell and you can't get it mended for a few days.		

CHAPTER 7
Only Connect

What do you say after you say Hello? (Eric Berne)

Most of us, in our daily lives, are bombarded with words, both written and spoken. We talk to our families, to colleagues at work, to neighbours over the garden wall, to friends as we walk, play squash, or have a meal with them, and to strangers as we buy a bus ticket, or a pound of fish. We make telephone calls to gossip or to talk business, or to make dental or hair appointments. We also watch television, see films, listen to the radio and read books. Advertisements try to sell us things we may or may not need, news and documentaries inform and, often, concern us, while fiction, fantasy and films allow us, in our imaginations, to enter worlds other than our own.

An Introduction to Communication

When you talk to or listen to people, facial expressions, gestures, tone of voice and demeanour, as well as the words used, all help to convey both the message and its meaning. When you feel misunderstood, then language can seem more like a chasm between you and other people, with neither side being able to bridge the gap. Sometimes, you may feel isolated and cut off from people, as though you are in a foreign country, where you cannot speak the language. Or you may, in new situations, feel unsure of yourself and not know what to say 'after you've said "hello"'.[1] Yet, when you feel understood, language can act as a bridge, enabling you to get the information you need, to get on with your work, to develop new friendships or to strengthen existing ones. The success or otherwise of our communication with others plays an important

61

part in our lives, and colours the content and quality of all our relationships with people.

Recognising *Parent*, *Adult* and *Child* in Communication

The Parent, Adult and Child framework presented in the earlier chapters can be used for understanding communication as well as personality. Each part of the personality can be recognised in action by the use of typical words, gestures and so on. As you become familiar with the framework, you can recognise the use of Parent, Adult or Child in your conversations, and become aware of any contradictions between the spoken word and the unspoken meaning. Words alone cannot always help you to identify which bit of the personality a person is using, but if you marry the words to the tone of voice, demeanour and so on, you can begin to identify whether Parent, Adult or Child is being used in communication. Some words tend to fit one part of the personality, whereas others might fit two or more parts. 'Want', for example, is often Child, whereas 'think'· is usually Adult, and 'ought' often Parent. On the other hand, 'I love you' might be a Child statement reflecting intimacy between lovers, or a nurturing Parent statement from a parent to a child. 'I'll do my best' when said in a firm tone of voice and with conviction is Adult, but when said in a whining, doubtful tone of voice is adapted Child.

When you are using your natural Child, you use words and phrases such as 'I want', 'give me', 'I feel', 'won't' or 'now'. Your tone of voice is happy, energetic, or enthusiastic. Your gestures, posture and so on are spontaneous, relaxed, or uninhibited. You are impulsive, creative, joyful or demanding in your behaviour.

When you are using your adapted Child, you use words and phrases such as 'thank you', 'please', 'I'll try', or 'can't'. Your tone of voice is placating, worried or angry. Your gestures, posture and so on are compliant, apologetic, sad, or aggressive. You conform, please others, or are depressed or rebellious in your behaviour.

When you are using your Adult, you use words and phrases such as 'that's interesting', 'I think', 'how', or 'why'. Your tone of voice is even, precise, calm or questioning. Your gestures, posture and so on are thoughtful, alert or open. You evaluate situations, collect and sift information and make decisions. You also mediate between Parent and Child.

When you are using your nurturing Parent, you use words and phrases such as 'take care', 'let me do that for you', 'good', or 'well done'. Your tone of voice is comforting, nurturing or concerned. Your gestures, posture and so on include smiles and touch, as you show concern and give comfort. You are caring, giving or loving in your behaviour, although you may be over-helpful at times.

When you are using your controlling Parent, you use words and phrases such as 'you should', 'I ought', 'must' or 'always'. Your tone of voice is firm, assertive, critical or judgmental. Your gestures, posture and so on include standing or sitting upright, frowns, a pointed finger, or folded arms. You are assertive, critical, authoritarian or controlling in your behaviour.

As well as using this framework to become attuned to the use of Parent, Adult and Child in yourself and others, you can also use it to help you understand the inter-action between yourself and other people. If a colleague consistently uses adapted Child language and behaviour, you may feel that, even though you really want to be using Adult to Adult forms of communication, you are being pushed into responding to him from either controlling or nurturing Parent. Conversely, if you tend to expect people to be critical of you, you won't hear things accurately, but will re-interpret what is said in order to make it fit in with your view of the world. If your boss, using Adult, says 'I'd like those figures by lunch-time', you might hear it as a critical statement from Parent, and tend to respond from adapted Child.

If you find yourself saying things your mother did, or using the same gestures as your father, you are likely to be using Parent, whereas if you find yourself responding to situations as you did when you were a child, you are likely to be using your natural or adapted Child. Sometimes, a particular event or situation can, in a sense, take you back to childhood, and your Child then relives all the excitement, elation or fear of the original experience.

Armed with these ideas, it becomes possible to analyse what goes on when we talk to each other and to understand why communication sometimes goes wrong, so that we end up feeling confused, misunderstood or on a different wavelength from the person we're talking with. There are basically three styles of communication, or transaction, between people: *open*, *crossed* and *double-level* or *ulterior*.

In order to understand these three styles, you need to think about which bit of your personality you and others would be using in the following imaginary conversations.

Open Communication

If you ask 'what's the time?' and the response is 'three o'clock', you are in Adult as you are asking the question. You would also expect to get, as you do in this example, an Adult response. If you wake up with a sore throat and temperature and say 'I do feel rotten' and the response is 'stay in bed and I'll bring you up a warm drink', your Child is looking for, and getting some Parent nurturing. If you're on the beach and you say 'race you into the sea' and the response is 'I'll beat you', you are both in Child.

In all these examples, only one part of the personality is used in each person, there are no hidden messages, nor are there any surprises. The person you talk to responds from the part of the personality that you expected to 'hit' with your statement. When this happens, it is usually possible for conversation to proceed smoothly.

Crossed Communication

Sometimes wires can get crossed, and you can finish up feeling uncomfortable, upset or misunderstood. If your Adult request to know the time is greeted with a critical Parent response of 'find out for yourself, stupid', your Child is liable to feel puzzled, hurt or angry. If your Child statement about feeling rotten is greeted with a Child response of 'so do I', then you are liable to feel that, instead of being looked after, you will have to look after someone else as well as yourself. If your natural Child request to race into the sea is greeted with 'you're too old for that sort of game', you may well feel squashed by the Parent of the person who is talking to you.

In these examples, two parts of the personality in each person have been used, and you will have been surprised by the response you got, as it doesn't come from the part you expected. It is also liable to push you into responding from a different part of your personality. Although conversation can continue when the wires get crossed like this, it may do so in a rather angry and negative way. Conversation is also very likely to break down in misunderstanding, anger or bewilderment.

Double-level or Ulterior Communication

Although the communication in these examples is not very successful, there are still no hidden or ulterior messages. When you get involved in ulterior communication with other people, you are giving or receiving a spoken message (often ostensibly Adult) as well as a hidden, unspoken message (often Child or Parent), with the hidden message being the real one. We are all aware of the double meanings in some of our everyday conversations, so that we read the apparently Adult invitation to 'come up and see my etchings' as really being a Child sexual one. If you replied 'thank you, I'd love to' in a flirtatious voice you would be replying to the hidden, but real message and not expecting to see etchings at all. If you say, in a childish, whining tone of voice 'I'd do the washing up, but I'm bound to smash things' you are apparently giving Adult information, but your Child's hidden message is 'aren't I stupid?' A critical sounding voice in response saying 'no thanks, I don't want my china smashed' also appears to give Adult information, but actually confirms your hidden Child's message about being stupid.

In these examples, two parts of the personality have been used in each person and, although the real message is hidden, it is often received and understood, so that there are not, in fact, any surprises. We learn to use these ulterior ways of communicating with others quite early in our lives. Sometimes, we use ulterior communication in ways that are socially acceptable and harmless—for example, when we use euphemisms, rather than direct statements. However, we often continue to use them because we fear conflict, or are involved in non-authentic relationships with people. Ulterior communication can also be used to keep us at arm's length from people and to reinforce negative images of ourselves.

Internal Communication

As has already been seen, you can also use this framework internally in order to sort out your own Child needs from your Parent opinions and values. It is important not to confuse the different parts of the personality, but to understand the difference between your thoughts, feelings and opinions. Sometimes, though, the Adult gets contaminated by scared Child feelings or Parent prejudice.

If, for example, you have a very real fear of getting cancer, you are likely to interpret every slight pain as the onset of the disease. You might appear to seek Adult information about this from your doctor, but as your Adult is really mixed up with your Child fears they, too, need calming. You can hear daily examples of Parent prejudice masquerading as Adult information as you listen to the news, and to the views of those political leaders who are intent on killing, imprisoning or otherwise harming people whose religion, politics or skin colour they dislike.

Effective Communication

At first sight it can seem that open communication is positive, whereas crossed and ulterior communication is negative.

This is not always entirely true—if you get very stuck in one part of your personality, you discover that, however clear and open you may wish to be, you have communication difficulties with people or find that your relationships are rather limited and limiting. If you tend, for example, to use Adult most of the time, you may well find that your inability to use Child and Parent when you need to do so is very restricting. Adult-to-Adult conversations may be fine at work, or if you want to know the time of a train, but they are not so useful if you need to take care of someone, or want to enjoy a close and loving relationship. Parent-to-Child conversations are ideal when you need looking after, but stultifying if you find yourself being looked after all the time, whether or not you need it.

Although crossed communication often does leave people feeling upset, misunderstood or puzzled, it is also a natural part of everyday conversation. In any situation where you discuss a range of topics, there will be many switches between Parent, Adult and Child, which you can usually accommodate quite easily. If you have been discussing finances on an Adult-to-Adult basis, you switch to Child as you decide it's time to have some fun and relaxation. After a brief cross as you move from Adult to Child, you might, after tea, cross back to Adult and continue the financial discussion, or you might seek some Parent support as you air your feelings about a frustrating or tiring day.

It can sometimes be useful to use a crossed communication quite deliberately in order to keep a discussion effective and open. One way of responding to a critical Parent comment which is designed to elicit your adapted Child, might be to stay firmly in your Adult, and refuse to budge into Child. At best, the person being critical will also move into Adult and give you reasoned information or criticism. At worst you, at least, will stay calmer and not end up with so many angry or irritated Child feelings.

In general, except for euphemisms, or the genuinely amusing element in jokes and puns, ulterior communication is not to be recommended. It works too much on assumption, and not enough on clear, open information. All too often, such communication is based on ignoring your needs and behaving as though all is well with the world when in reality you are feeling scared, unhappy or vulnerable. If you are not honest with yourself, or with others, you are liable to lose touch with your real self and to become involved in 'games playing' or non-authentic behaviour. This more extensive use of ulterior communication will be discussed more fully in Chapter 9.

I realise that there are times when, in order not to hurt feelings, or to avoid conflict, we are not entirely honest, but in my view the more we can be honest in our relationships, the more we are likely to be able to deal constructively with conflict, and the better able we will be to enjoy relaxed, close and loving relationships.

If your communication with others is clear and open, you will rarely get involved in this ulterior style of communication. But if you tend to do so, you may need to ask yourself what prevents you from being clearer and more open. Unmet needs and hidden resentments have a habit of festering, rather than going away, and they can turn into unpleasant arguments, aggression, depression, or psychosomatic illness.

If on the other hand you find yourself on the receiving end of such communication, you can deal with it in a variety of ways. You can listen for the hidden message and try to bring it into the open. An example of bringing hidden messages into the open might occur if, faced with the kind of aggressive, angry or even jokey conversation which can often cover up fear or apprehension, you bring the hidden fears into the open, enabling people to talk about their real needs.

Secondly, you can encourage people to move into open Adult communication, rather than ulterior communication. If someone is using a helpless, adapted Child masquerading as Adult, to try to manipulate you into doing something for them, you can encourage them to move into Adult by refusing to be drawn into being a nurturing Parent, although your Parent might well need to acknowledge their Child feelings as you try to get them to use their Adult.

Thirdly, if you are faced with people using their negative controlling Parent, you don't have to respond from anxious or eager-to-please Child, even though this is what they want. You can respond from Adult with information; from nurturing Parent if you think they are covering up anxious feelings underneath their Parent bluster; from your own positive controlling Parent if you think you need to confront their attitudes to you; or from Child if you think you could engage them in some fun and relaxation.

Perhaps the main key to good communication is the ability truly to listen to others. All too often conversation proceeds as though it were on two separate tracks, with both sides talking, but neither side listening, as the following extract from Elspeth Huxley's *Flame Trees of Thika* [2] shows:

'Thank goodness you're safe,' Robin said ... 'I have missed you ... I'm planting out coffee and everyone is hard at it, and the office work has got chaotic, and Sammy is away.'

'It's lovely to see you,' Tilly responded. 'And you look well. ... Do you know I shot a lion: not a very large one, but definitely a lion: the skin is coming on with the safari, so we shan't need another rug in the living-room.'

'I've got the still in good working order, except for one or two small details, and I think we shall be able to start on the geraniums in a week or two if this rain keeps on.'

'In a way I didn't want to shoot it, but it sloped off into a donga, and when I saw something tawny moving in the grass I let fly and hit it in the leg.'

Understanding what happens when you talk to other people can help you make better sense of the situations you meet in your day-to-day life, and to realise why, sometimes, apparently normal conversations turn sour. Using your Parent, Adult and Child flexibly, avoiding ulterior communication and keeping crossed wires to a minimum, being open in your dealings with people, while being sensitive to the real messages they are passing to you, is probably the best way of avoiding communication tangles in your day-to-day life. Finally, develop the art of truly active listening. Active listening means you focus on what other people are saying, rather than on what you are going to reply, or on responding with your experiences. In other words, conversations become a true dialogue, rather than two monologues.

Awareness Exercise

There is an opportunity to explore your style of communication more fully in Exercise 5 in Chapter 11. This exercise gives you a chance to practise recognising the parts of the personality that people use in day-to-day conversations. Look at the conversations below and imagine the tone of voice being used, then write down which parts of the personality (+NP, −NP, +CP, −CP, A, +NC, −NC, +AC, −AC) you think are being used. Sometimes, the statement can be said in more than one way, so you may well have more than one possible response.

1. You should hear what Jack said about Jane—it'll curl your toes.
2. There are several errors in this letter.
3. There you go again, always arriving late.
4. Why must I eat my cabbage, Daddy doesn't?
5. You should read this book—you'll have a really good cry.
6. I think young people have far too much freedom these days.
7. What about taking a day off and going to the coast?
8. Do you call that making the bed properly?
9. The car has broken down again—I could scream.
10. You look awful. Let me make you a cup of tea.
11. You're always ill on Mondays—I call it 'Mondayitis' not illness.
12. You look really great.
13. It looks as though it will rain—take a coat with you.
14. A pound of apples, please—make sure they're not bruised.
15. Don't worry about me, I'll be alright.

CHAPTER 8
Your Script gets Written

*While living in the present ... take from the past what
the past offers of living value* (Gilbert Phelps)

Earlier chapters have presented an outline of personality development; this chapter fills in the details by looking more fully at early influences on present behaviour. As adults, our behaviour is guided by the demands, interests and pleasures of our individual lifestyles—earning a living, pursuing hobbies, enjoying family life and friendships. For many of us, particularly in our rapidly changing and mobile society, our lives today may seem to have little connection with our childhood, or even with earlier stages of our adult life. Yet, although we may have discarded many of our former beliefs and attitudes, we are still very much the product, not merely of our own particular set of genes, but of our time, our culture and, at a more individual level, our personal history.

The Formation of the Script

Parents, among others, are the people who teach us what is acceptable behaviour in both the family and the environment in which we live. Behaviour is based on the attitudes we develop and the beliefs we hold about ourselves and others. Although much of what we learn about values, attitudes and behaviour is not at a conscious level, we develop, from a very early age, ideas about who we are and what we want to be or to do with our lives. It is as though, as we set out on a journey into the unknown, our parents are sending us a series of messages or handy hints they think will guide us on our way. We then use these messages to make a plan to help us decide how we might,

71

in general terms, live our lives. Although we know that circumstances both within and outside our control may alter the plan, most of us feel the need for some sort of structure. Thus, the experiences we have, the messages we receive, and the decisions we make form our own individual *script* or *life plan*.

As has already been seen, parental behaviour provides a model for children to copy. Children also pick up, both from what their parents say, and from what they do and how they do it, how they are expected to behave. Whereas these expectations are rarely, if ever, given as precise or succint messages, it becomes possible, as you think about the beliefs and attitudes you hold now, to translate these into short, often pithy phrases which reflect very accurately the original message you received.

Sometimes the messages are positive. They give you *permissions* that encourage you to like yourself, to develop your personality fully and to grow up as a 'good enough' person. Sometimes the messages are restrictive or destructive, or your misunderstanding or re-interpretation of positive messages turns them into a negative influence. They act as prohibitions or *injunctions* and stunt your emotional growth and development, so that you grow up with a sense that somehow you are never good enough, either for yourself or for others.

Permissions Needed for Healthy Development

All children need a number of basic permissions in order to grow up emotionally, as well as physically, healthy. The first and most important permission is 'to exist'. Children who are wanted and loved by their parents get such a permission, whereas children who are ignored, or told that 'if it weren't for you, I wouldn't be in this awful marriage' or 'we didn't want you, anyway', get a 'don't exist' message.

Children whose parents are relaxed about both their bodies and their feelings get a permission that 'it's OK to feel' (both bodily sensations and emotions). In such families, for example, nakedness is not giggled about or frowned on, toilet training is relaxed, and affection is freely and openly given and received.

Children who get a 'don't feel' message grow up in families where, for example, nakedness is considered rude or dirty, where their toilet training is strict and they are punished from an early age for wet or dirty pants, and where affection is rationed or non-existent.

Children also need permission to think. Children who are encouraged to work things out for themselves, and who get appropriate support while they are doing so, grow up with a permission 'to think'. Conversely, children who are discouraged from finding things out, whose questions are ignored or who are over-protected, grow up with a 'don't think' message.

As well as being able to show feelings, children need permission to 'be close'. Children whose parents have open and trusting relationships with each other and with other people learn to trust others and to feel good about emotional and physical closeness. This is particularly important in terms of teaching children about the opposite sex. Teaching girls that 'men only want one thing' or boys that 'all women want is a meal ticket' encourages mistrust and misunderstandings between men and women. Children who are given these sorts of messages, as well as learning that they can't trust people, get a 'don't be close' message from their parents.

Children also need permission to be themselves, and to be their age. They need to be loved for being the sex they are, the age they are and for their own particular personalities and talents. When they are encouraged to follow their own interests, and when their development is neither forced, like a hot-house plant, nor repressed, they get 'be yourself' and 'be your age' permissions. Girls who are told 'we really wanted a boy' or boys who are encouraged to 'be like daddy' get a 'don't be you' message. Sometimes, parents force their children to grow up too quickly. Where, for example, parents separate, or one partner dies, older children might feel they have to grow up and 'be the man (or woman) of the house'. Conversely, parents might love their children as babies, but not feel able to cope with their changing demands as they grow older. They keep them in babyish clothes, such as short trousers, and in a variety of other ways discourage their growing independence. In both these examples, children get a 'don't be your age' message.

Children also need permission to succeed. Those whose achievements are recognised, who are given support and encouragement as they pursue their interests and enjoy their successes, get a 'you can succeed' permission. But those whose achievements are ignored or discounted, or who get little encouragement to develop their interests, get a 'don't succeed' message.

I find, when people come for therapy, that in nearly every case, they have incorporated messages from their parents that are destructive or restrictive. For example, Alan's mother used to talk about drowning him as she would kittens. Perhaps not surprisingly, Alan has grown up feeling hurt and depressed by this early message and, in counselling, needs to accept a new permission that it's fine for him to exist and to get on with his life.

Carol was encouraged to be good and not to feel. When she was ill, she was encouraged to 'snap out of it', with the result that, as a grown- up, she has repressed many of her feelings. She is now allowing herself to experience all her feelings, including sad or unhappy ones, so that she can make more effective decisions and be more fully in touch with herself.

Messages are Usually Mixed

We all have our own particular mixture of dos and don'ts with most of us usually receiving a mixture of positive and negative messages. Your parents may have encouraged you to 'enjoy life', 'be happy', 'enjoy being a woman/man', 'save for a rainy day', 'get married and have a family', 'have a career', and so on. Negative messages may not be passed so openly, but you may also have received restrictive messages such as 'don't have fun', 'don't trust men/women/people', 'don't think of yourself', 'don't ever get angry', 'don't expect much from life', and so on.

John learnt that it was acceptable to show his feelings, to do well, to think for himself, to be a boy, and so on. At the same time, he also felt that he had messages about not being wanted, about having to grow up too fast and about being as his parents wanted him to be. As a result, he is in a confused and unhappy state, wanting to resist being forced into the mould his parents have chosen for him, yet being undecided about what he wants for himself. As he begins to explore his feelings, he is beginning to use his own Adult to decide which of the messages from the past he needs to keep and which he needs to jettison.

Sometimes Behaviour Can Feel Driven

Sometimes the messages may seem to be positive, and indeed socially acceptable, but they can have an unpleasant sting in their tail. These are *driver messages* that make us feel that we don't, in a sense, have control over our behaviour. It is as though the message drives us on, regardless of what we feel we want to do. *Hurry up*, *be perfect*, *try hard*, *please others (not yourself)* and *be strong* are said to be the five major messages that are likely to result in a sensation of being driven, rather than being in the driving seat yourself.

Sometimes, doing things quickly can be positive. If you are performing a boring, but necessary chore, such as cleaning the bath, or you have a train to catch or a deadline to meet, hurrying up might well be essential or useful. By the same token, if you are forever rushing, always with too much to do, and if you feel guilty or anxious if you stop, then you might be suffering from a *hurry up driver*. Your symptoms would be that you don't allow yourself fully to enjoy the process of what you are doing, to enjoy a relaxed time with people or to value giving time to yourself. If you suffer from hurrying up, an alternative, and more useful, message for you to take on now might be *it's alright to take your time*. You can add any riders of your own that you like, such as '... when it's appropriate', or '... and to enjoy what you do', or '... and to leave things undone sometimes' or 'and to relax and feel good about it'.

Although I have become more aware of and less driven by the negative aspects of my own hurry up message, I am aware that it hasn't entirely disappeared. I know that my hurry up is in full swing when I begin to say to myself, 'I haven't got time to go for a swim', or I fail to take a break when I am working hard at my word processor, or I rush about on what a friend describes as my 'frenetic days' trying to do several things at once.

Being perfect is sometimes crucial. In surgery, engineering and so on, precision, accuracy and getting it right may well save lives. If you undergo an operation, you want to know that the surgeon is dealing with the right bit of you, and not just making a reasonably accurate guess about where to make the incision. When you drive over a bridge, you would be unhappy if you felt the engineers hadn't bothered to be too precise in working out stress, load-bearing and so on. It is possible to enjoy a sense of perfection in all sorts of everyday events—balancing a ledger, making a cake, enjoying a summer's day. If on the other hand you strive to be perfect in all you do, or in yourself, you are giving yourself an impossible job in which you are doomed to fail, as no one can achieve perfection all the time. You are likely to spend a good deal of time criticising yourself and, perhaps, others for not living up to your expectations. A more useful message might be *it's alright to make mistakes and to learn from them* or *I'm good enough to feel good about myself.*

Sheila finds herself in a real dilemma, as she believes she ought to be perfect, yet knows that she isn't. She has a belief that other people are more perfect than her, so she is always on the lookout for someone on whom to model herself. Yet if she tries to do this, because she's not being herself, she fails (in her eyes) once more and the vicious circle then begins all over again. Sheila is still struggling with the idea that it is possible just to be herself, without having to be perfect.

Trying hard also has its uses. Achievement does not always come easily, and you may have to work very hard in order to learn new skills or overcome the obstacles between yourself and what you wish to achieve. Accepting failure with a good grace is also a useful ability to possess. But if, for some reason, you really feel that you can never succeed, or you tend to give up before your possible success, then you are likely to suffer from a *try hard driver*. You might find it more fun and more challenging to change your belief to one that *you can succeed*. You can stop being among 'those victims of Nature who fill their lives with unnecessary misfortune'.[1]

Pleasing others is a very necessary human attribute. There is a very real pleasure to be gained from making a meal for friends, or taking the trouble to buy a gift that you know will suit someone's tastes or interests. When you put your own needs or your tiredness in the background because you have to take care of a small child, or look after someone who is ill, or help a colleague out at work, then pleasing others is appropriate. If for whatever reason you tend to spend all your time pleasing others, or fearing others' disapproval if you don't, you are liable, as has been suggested earlier, to become bitter,

Of course I care about your awful day, but I'm afraid you don't live here

resentful, depressed or ill. If you can learn to *please others, as well as yourself*, you may find that both you and the people around you are happier.

Len had a history of falling violently in love usually—as he realised with hindsight—with unsuitable women. When he was in the throes of being in love, much of his time and energy was spent trying to please the woman in his life, often ignoring his own needs and interests in the process. When not in love, he had lost sight of knowing how to please himself, and was merely miserable, lonely and unhappy. Len gradually began to spend more time doing the things he enjoyed, such as developing and nurturing other friendships, in order to get a better balance in his *please others* message. By the time he'd finished counselling, he had a much stronger sense of his own worth. He feels a happier and nicer person generally and enjoys his life more fully, whether or not he is with the woman in his life.

Being strong can be essential when crises occur, or you have to face emotional or practical difficulties. The ability to stay calm, or to to be able to draw on your internal resources, helps you either to take appropriate action or gradually to find ways of dealing with the hurt and of recovering. If on the other hand you feel you should never appear vulnerable, or ask for help, or show your feelings, then being strong might well mean that people get the wrong impression about you. They may fail to notice when you are in fact, 'not waving, but drowning'.[2] If you can begin to accept that *it's alright to ask for help*, again adding, if you wish, your own riders, such as 'when I need it' or 'from people who care about me' or 'without losing my own strengths', then you may well find that you feel more relaxed in yourself, and that you get closer to others.

The Impact of Messages

The impact of the messages you received when you were young depended on their *source*, *type*, *intensity*, *timing*, *consistency* and *frequency*. Messages from parents are likely to be far more powerful than messages from people who are less important in your life. Negative messages, such as 'I hate you', or 'you're clumsy' are often more intense in their impact than positive ones, hence the tendency, in some people, to remember these more vividly. Early messages, given when you had only a limited knowledge about the world outside the home, are liable to be more powerful than later ones, which can be set against other kinds of information. If you were consistently told that you were loved and valued, you are more likely to believe this than if you got mixed messages from parents who blew hot and cold, smothering you with affection one day and ignoring you the next. Messages that are frequently repeated are more liable to be accepted than the occasional, throwaway message.

If you have generally received a package of positive messages, then the script you will be living out for yourself will be a constructive one. You will be getting on with your life, while taking responsibility for your actions, and dealing positively with problems as they occur. You will have a concern for the world you live in, for those you care about, and for yourself.

If you have received a mix of messages, with positive and negative ones fairly equally balanced, or with some messages conflicting with others, you may find that your life has far more ups and downs. You may find that you play safe, or swing from one extreme to the other as you obey first the positive messages then the negative ones.

If you have received, in the main, negative messages or have lost sight of positive ones you were given, you may find that you are one of life's losers, or victims. Being a loser or a victim in the sense in which I am using it here, means carrying into the present not what is of value from your past, but the obsolete, inaccurate, hurtful messages that do you more harm than good. I am not talking about the many people who are victims of circumstances beyond their control, such as the poor and the unemployed, but those who seem almost deliberately to get into financial, relationship or other difficulties.

The permissions and injunctions you received when you were young come to form the basis of your beliefs, attitudes and behaviour. In order to reinforce these beliefs and messages, a sort of circular pattern can be set up as you grow up, and you behave in ways that convince you that these early messages are true, accurate or correct. In this way these early messages continue to influence you, unless you decide to make some real changes in the present. Chapter 9, therefore, looks at the ways in which this reinforcement occurs.

Discovering Your Script

Although Exercise 6 in Chapter 11 gives you a chance to explore your script more fully, the statements below give you a chance to begin identifying the messages you have received from your parents. You need to consider what they told you about yourself, how you should behave, what you should believe and so on.

Think first about the permissions you received, and then about any negative messages or injunctions. Although it is best to go as far back as you can remember in order to get in touch with the earliest, and possibly the most powerful messages, if you can't do this try to concentrate on those you can remember, at whatever age. You might have received messages about the following for instance:

1. Your worth—whether you were wanted and loved for yourself.
2. Your skills, talents and abilities.
3. Your femininity or masculinity (whichever is appropriate).
4. Your sexuality.
5. Your intelligence or cleverness.
6. Your physical appearance and attractiveness.
7. Your spiritual self, e.g. religious or other philosophical beliefs.
8. Your health.
9. Whether you should marry and have children.
10. Whether you should have a career and, if so, what it might be.
11. Whether you were like anyone, e.g. an uncle, and if so, what this meant in terms of what you were like as a person.
12. Being successful.
13. Being happy.
14. Being yourself.
15. Enjoying life.
16. How you would end up.

This is by no means an exhaustive list, and you may well have messages about many other aspects of your life and personality, e.g. 'work hard', 'do your duty', 'do better than us', 'get on with people'. Brainstorm as many ideas as you can before moving on to the relevant exercise in Chapter 11.

CHAPTER 9

Spending Your Time

Live all you can; it's a mistake not to (Henry James)

Development of Attitudes to Self and Others

None of us ever sees the world as it really is. We see it through a set of perceptions, based on our individual backgrounds, values and beliefs, about what is real or true. It is as though we translate our experiences into our own language to make it fit into our view of the world. This model of personality proposes *four basic positions*, or sets of perceptions, that we can take towards ourselves and others.

Liking Self and Others

Firstly, you can be emotionally healthy, autonomous and a good enough person, *liking yourself and others*. You are capable of making close and loving relationships with others; you use your skills and talents constructively, and you are ethical and responsible, as well as spontaneous and open in your behaviour. You 'live all you can' and get on with your life, rather than sighing over a regretted past, or fearing an unknown future.

Getting on with life does not mean that you are perfect. Neither does it mean that you never have days when things go wrong, or you feel tired, irritable or sad. But when things do go wrong, you tackle them constructively; when you feel tired, you take care of yourself; when you feel irritable, you track down the source and deal with it; when you feel sad because of some life event, you acknowledge it and give yourself time to grieve.

If you are getting on with your life in general you are likely to have had good experiences when you were young which gave you a positive sense of yourself. Or, if this was not the case, to have made some constructive changes in your beliefs and lifestyle as you grew up.

Liking Self but not Others

Secondly, you seem to *like yourself, but not others*. You are suspicious and mistrustful of other people, often seeing them as being responsible when things go wrong in your life. But, even though you may appear to be self-confident, often in an aggressive or blustering way, your apparently confident exterior usually hides a sad, unhappy person, who is busily building defences against the world. You can be a martyr who is always being put upon by others, a victim for whom things are always going wrong, or a loner who can't trust people enough to get close to them. You believe that if you keep yourself to yourself or you don't trust people, you will be able to get on with your life without being hurt or let down by them.

This position is taken on in childhood as a way of dealing with emotional hurt, being let down, being moved around and cared for by different people, or being unwanted. Children whose need for attention, love and nurturing is ignored survive by deciding that they must take care of themselves but, in order to do so, they shut themselves off from others. As adults, people in this position reinforce their early decisions by continuing to believe that they can't trust or get close to others. Thus, what might have been a good survival strategy in an unhappy childhood becomes, in adulthood, a strait-jacket in which people live isolated lives, putting much of their energy into convincing themselves that they are happy that way.

Liking Others but not Self

Thirdly, you may *not like yourself very much but see others as better than you*. You may feel depressed and helpless about yourself, and try to find someone else to look after you. You may well believe that, if you can find Mr or Ms Right, everything in your life will be fine. If this is so you are liable to make so many demands on others that, sooner or later, relationships break down, and you are then left with seeking out someone else to take care of you, or with facing your own sense of depression.

This position is taken on in childhood, as a way of dealing with persistent negative messages. If children are constantly belittled, told they are useless, stupid, clumsy and so on, their sense of self develops negatively, rather than positively. It is difficult for children to know that what they are being told is not necessarily true, but based on other people's values. They tend to believe that if they are said to be no good, then it must be true, and they learn to feel depressed and not 'good enough'. As adults, people in this position reinforce these early decisions by replaying the negative messages internally so that they continue to feel depressed and unhappy. What was difficult to refute as a child because they had no other information becomes for them a prison of depression from which they feel they can't escape.

Disliking Self and Others

Finally, you may *not like either yourself or others* and may live out a destructive life, disliking and devaluing both yourself and other people, and being sad, depressed, mistrustful and unhappy.

This position is taken on in childhood, as a way of dealing with severe physical or emotional abuse. Children who are ill-treated come to believe that they are no good, and, as a way of making sense of what is happening to them, also learn to mistrust others. This may have been a realistic assessment then, but holding this belief as an adult results in people in this position leading isolated, depressed, often destructive lives, in which they neither like themselves nor like or trust others.

Most people who come for therapy have, at least at that particular time in their lives, a negative view of themselves, using phrases such as 'I don't like myself' or 'I feel I'm no good'.

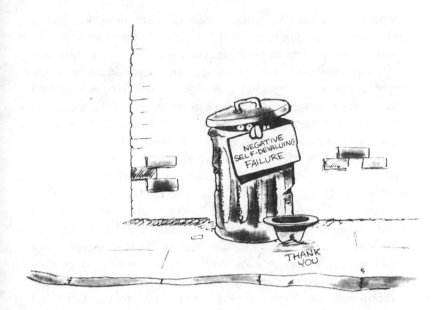

Katie decided to seek some counselling after a workshop in which she found, when asked to describe five things she liked about herself, that she could think of none. By the time our contact ended, Katie had made several significant changes in her life. Not only did she feel much more positive about herself, but she had gained an 'A' level and been offered a place at university as a mature student. She had ended a destructive relationship, and developed a number of good, loving friendships. She was much more in touch with her own feelings and needs and spent more time taking care of these as well as having time and energy for her friends. Most significantly of all, when Katie had a subsequent health problem, she saw it as a temporary setback, rather than allowing it to undermine her new-found sense of self-worth.

Different Feelings for Different Aspects of Self

You may find that although in most respects you get on with your life, you feel depressed about one particular aspect, such as your appearance or your work. Instead of using the good feelings you have about yourself to help change your attitudes or behaviour to this area of your life, you may for instance reinforce it with an unhealthy diet, or by ignoring possible options that might be available to you in terms of your work. Or you may find that as long as things go well you can get on with life, but that, if you have a problem to deal with, you slip into one of the other positions rather than dealing with it constructively.

Finally, you may have a preferred set of perceptions on which you base your life. The following would possibly be a typical day for a person who tends to be depressed a good deal of the time. He wakes up on a cold, wet day and feels depressed about having to go to work in such weather and decides to have a bit longer in bed. He then finds that in the rush to get ready the toast burns and the milk boils over, for which he blames himself. He misses the train and is late for work, where he gets a reprimand which provides external reinforcement for his sense of depression. He then further reinforces it by making some silly mistakes in his work, and by having a row with his partner, a colleague or a friend at the end of the day. Consequently he recycles his feelings of depression all day, and ends up feeling isolated and unhappy.

Ways and Styles of Spending Time

You reinforce the perceptions you hold about yourself and others in a variety of ways, including the ways in which you spend your time. Transactional analysis theory classifies ways of spending time into six categories. I differ slightly from this in that I classify the ways into four categories. These are *withdrawing from people*, *rituals*, *pastimes*, and *activities*. Each of these can be used in either one of two styles — the *authentic* style, and the *non-authentic* or *games-playing* style.

The Authentic Style

Although withdrawal, rituals, pastimes and activities encompass much of our day-to-day activity, the relationships we make also affect the way we spend our time. *Intimacy and authenticity* in relationships occur when people have a relationship of openness, trust, affection or love. When such a relationship occurs between lovers, inside or outside marriage, the intimacy also includes sexual and sensual love. Intimacy in the sense in which I am using it here is not confined to such relationships, but includes parent–child love, the affection of relatives and friends, or close working relationships, particularly those where colleagues are relied on for one's own safety, such as mining or mountaineering.

The Non-authentic Style

Conversely, when we are involved in *games-playing* relationships, we use ways of relating that reinforce negative beliefs about ourselves and others. As has already been seen, some families encourage their children to repress positive aspects of their personality. Sometimes, open communication is frowned upon and the family members develop ulterior ways of communicating with each other. In other words, the children gradually develop a range of non-authentic feelings, styles of communication and behaviours, and they then use these automatically, whether or not they are appropriate. As a result such children learn to use games-playing styles of relating to other people.

When you play *games*, you use ulterior or double-level communication, but eventually you make a switch, so that you bring the game into the open but still finish up feeling bad. For example, someone who believes that 'nobody really loves me' will play games in relationships in order to reinforce this belief.

Games are played from the role of being a *victim*, a *persecutor* or a *rescuer*. If you believe that both the world and other people conspire against you, or you find that things are always going wrong, you are a *victim*—you make a habit of getting into relationships and situations where you are always being let down, or taken advantage of in some way. If you are overly critical of others, always looking for, and finding fault, you are a *persecutor*—you keep people at a distance or get into relationships in which you keep control, and in which there is little real affection. If you spend all your time caring for others, and being over-nurturing, you are a *rescuer*—you seek out people to look after, but become depressed and resentful at being on the endless treadmill of caring for others, at the expense of yourself. Whatever your favourite role, you are liable to switch to others from time to time. The victim may, for example, persecute others when he is blaming them for his own misfortunes. The persecutor may rescue others when, having been very controlling or hurtful, she attempts to make amends. The rescuer may become the victim when the help he offers is rejected, and he is left feeling let down.

When games are being played in relationships, people may choose one of two possible options. They may either look for someone who complements their own personality or for someone with a similiar personality with whom they can compete. If, as a child, you had your Adult and Parent restricted, you will tend to want to be looked after, and you are liable to look for someone with a large Parent and Adult of their own who can do this. Or you might look for someone else with a large Child, so that you can have a lot of fun together. If this is the case neither of you will have a well developed Adult or Parent, and you could find yourself either competing unsuccessfully with your partner for nurturing or seeking out someone else to make decisions for you.

Games, like pastimes, have been given names. If you play *yes, but*, you seek advice but reinforce feeling helpless by rejecting all the advice you are given and then believing that your problems are insoluble. If you play *harried* you are always in a rush, often filling your time with things you don't enjoy doing, and never giving yourself time to relax or to have any fun. If you play *I'm only trying to help you*, you rush around being helpful to people, and then feel upset and hurt when they reject your help. You may find you play one of the many named games, or you may find that you have developed some games of your own. In either case, you play games as a way of trying to get needs met in an ulterior, non-authentic way.

I recently had a day in which I nearly ended up playing *poor me* and feeling a real victim, but, fortunately, a sense of humour finally rescued me from too much self-pity. After a weekend away, I found that my car wouldn't start due to my running down the battery by having left something on. I began to feel stressed, as it took two hours for the rescue services to arrive thus forcing me to cancel several tutorials. I finally arrived at the university, with an hour or so to spare before I was due to do some teaching. I decided to relax by having lunch in a nearby park, only to have a grey squirrel jump on my knee, steal my sandwich and bite my finger. As I crossed the road to the university, after checking that I didn't need a tetanus jab, a motorbike went through the red traffic-lights and nearly knocked me down. When I finally arrived home, I found the central heating had broken down and the house was very cold. By this time, I was feeling particularly sorry for myself and could easily have drifted into the 'poor me' game, but I then realised that, in fact, things weren't really so bad. After all, the car hadn't been stolen, and was now working, I didn't have any after-effects from the squirrel bite, I hadn't actually been run over, and the central heating breakdown was only a breakdown, not a gas leak with the house being blown up.

Ways of Spending Time

Withdrawing in an authentic style from what is going on around you affords the opportunity for reflection, for recharging emotional batteries or for creative work. It can occur through such activities as day-dreaming, meditating, listening to music or when going for a walk. You may also withdraw from contact with people because you feel negative towards them. When this happens, you may be using a games-playing style of behaving. You may become emotionally starved of recognition and attention from others, and this may reinforce a sense of unhappiness or depression within yourself.

In *rituals*, you are involved in predictable ways of behaving in which the rules are known. Again you may use either authentic or games-playing styles of behaving. Some rituals are simple, short contacts, such as the standard daily exchange you might have about the weather as you buy your newspaper; others are complex cultural rituals, such as those to do with birth, marriage and death. Weddings, for example, whether simple or elaborate, Christian, Jewish, Hindu or Muslim, all have their stylised, ritualistic elements which are known and understood by people within that culture or religion. Rituals can be extremely valuable, as they can act as a first step in helping you to get to know your colleagues in a new job, or your neighbours when you move to a new town. They can also give you a sense of belonging and of rootedness in your own culture. But if much of your life is based on rituals and superficial contact, they can be used as a way of keeping your distance from people, maintaining games-playing styles of relating and of reinforcing negative life positions.

When you are involved in *pastimes*, you talk about such things as clothes, cars and sport. Eric Berne gave pastimes various names: *ain't it awful* is played about the weather, the score in the test match, the state of the country and so on. *Wardrobe*

She's ve-ry comfortable. 150 miles per gallon of water—on a good run of course. And the price they charge for the old H_2O these days ...

deals with talk about the latest fashions, and the clothes you've bought (or might like to buy), *general motors* is all about comparing makes of car, engine power, acceleration and so on. Pastimes are more open-ended than rituals, but are also useful in new situations, or in social or work gatherings where you don't know people well. As with rituals, they can be used as a springboard for authentic relationships, or as a way of keeping conversation and relationships superficial.

Activities enable you to deal with the daily demands of the world. You are involved in activities when you earn your living, do the housework, or are engaged in your social interests or hobbies. If you feel that you are a 'good enough' person, you use your talents to the full. And, in your contact with others, whether it is at work, an evening class, a society connected with a hobby, with family or friends, you are an authentic person. If you are games-playing in your contacts with people, you use work, hobbies, friendships and family life as the places where you can play your games and further your negative beliefs about yourself and others.

For all of us, daily life has some tedious, dull elements—fixing a dripping tap, doing the ironing, cleaning the bath. We have numerous superficial contacts which are not likely to lead to intimacy—chatting to a stranger on a train, doing the shopping in a supermarket, asking someone for directions. We also live in a culture in which saving time is seen to be a virtue and wasting time a sin, but in reality we can neither save time nor waste it, we can only spend it and live it. An awareness of the value of spending time enjoyably, productively and authentically can in fact help us to sort out priorities in our lives, to avoid games in our relationships with others and to increase the time spent in intimacy.

The focus so far has been mainly on making sense of behaviour rather than change. The final chapters provide some ideas about making changes in attitudes, feelings and behaviour.

Naming the Game

Exercises 7 and 8 in Chapter 11 give you a chance to look at your perceptions of yourself and others, and at the ways and styles of passing time that you adopt. Some of the better-known games identified by Berne are listed below. See whether you can recognise either yourself and/or other people whom you know.

Name	Theme
Name	*Theme*
1. Harried	'I'm too busy to take a break'.
2. Kick me	'I'm always doing things wrong'.

3.	Wooden leg	'How can I help it, with my background'.
4.	Poor me	'No one has got as many problems as me'.
5.	Yes, but	'Yes, but I've tried that already …'.
6.	I'm only trying to help	'People always let me down, although I'm only trying to help'.
7.	Blemish	'I'm always having to bail others out'.
8.	Rapo	'You can't trust men/women'.
9.	Frigid	'Not tonight, I've got a headache'.
10.	If it weren't for you	'If it weren't for you, I could do such a lot with my life'.
11.	If only	'If only I had more money/better looks/a more understanding partner … life would be fine'.
12.	See what you made me do	'You made me do it … I didn't want to'.

CHAPTER 10

A Change for the Better

Self-knowledge is an essential preliminary to self-change (Aldous Huxley)

The emphasis in previous chapters has been on understanding the impact of early experiences on present-day attitudes, beliefs and behaviour. The blueprint provided can also be used to help you make better sense of your own and others' behaviour, and to manage everyday situations more effectively.

For example, if you want to make a complaint about something, such as faulty goods, using the Adult assertively, rather than an angry, critical Parent or an over-apologetic adapted Child, is most likely to produce a reasonable response. If you are aware that you tend to be over-nurturing you can, on occasions, hold back and leave it to others to take some responsibility for caring and organising. If you get into a game, you can refuse to play it or you can try to identify and meet the hidden need. If you become aware of the way in which out-of-date beliefs interfere with current reality, you can begin to throw these out in favour of new ones which are more attuned to the present situation.

Resisting Perfection

There has also been an emphasis on the idea of the good enough person. One of the dangers of focusing on changes in behaviour, attitudes, or feelings is that you can still fall into the 'being perfect' trap, particularly as this is very much encouraged by the culture in which we live. You might stop trying to be superwoman, or superman, or the best salesman, or top accountant but you might instead just try to be the perfect personality. Instead of getting rid of archaic beliefs and attitudes, you might merely swop them for new ones in which you strive for an unattainable perfection.

If you decide instead to concentrate on being good enough, you will not only like yourself and others, but can begin to recognise your own and their fallibility. You take care of your own needs, but forgive yourself on the days when you don't do this so well. You respond to everyday events appropriately, but recognise that, sometimes, archaic beliefs and attitudes might interfere with this process. You make mistakes, but learn from them. You see other people as real, rather than through a stereotyped view, and are also aware of the prejudices you might have. You have an ethical base from which you care about wider issues such as the environment, nuclear power and so on, but you do not blame yourself for your inability to change the world. You have fun and enjoy life, people and the world around you, but you do so without harming yourself or others. If you do face difficulties, you look for information and options that will, as far as possible, help you to resolve, ameliorate or manage them.

We live in a world which is rapidly changing and in which we are encouraged, through advertising and so on, to want or need more goods, better relationships, fantastic sex lives, amazing holidays and so on. Magazines encourage us to produce better dinner parties, to wear smarter clothes, or to buy faster cars. They encourage us to feel that our tried and tested steak and kidney pie, or comfortable old coat, or serviceable, but old, car aren't good enough. Advertising encourages us to plan summer holidays on warm beaches during the winter, or to think about buying Christmas cards and presents before the autumn has even set in. Sayings such as 'the grass is greener on the other side', 'keeping up with the Jones's' and so on tend to reinforce a sense of dissatisfaction with life as it is.

We need not in any way oppose change as such, or the excitement and pleasure of new clothes or a car, the usefulness of labour-saving devices, or the cutting down of tedious chores. However, change does need to be a real plus and should enhance our ability to live more fully in the present. This applies equally to changes in attitudes and behaviour. Deciding that your natural Child has been neglected is fine, but then concentrating all your energy on having fun, regardless of the effect on others, your bank balance and your work or family responsibilities is not 'a change for the better'.

Deciding What to Change

If you do think you want to make some changes in your life, it is important, before you do so, to be fully aware of all the things in your own personality and in your present lifestyle that are positive, and to make sure you keep these. You will find, in any case, that unless you really want to make changes and are committed to them fully, they won't happen. Something will always ensure that you put off the change until tomorrow, or fail to achieve it. But if you should decide you want to make some changes, it is useful to follow some basic guidelines.

You need, first and foremost, to believe that change is possible. Alongside this, you need to be aware that it normally occurs in small steps, often slowly, and sometimes falteringly. Jane Gardam[1] describes this beautifully when she says:

> 'It is usually just fancy when you say that "someone changed from that moment". … Often the intention is definable—the moment when we say "from now on I shall do this, do that". But the change itself proceeds waveringly—and of course often does not proceed at all. But changes—huge changes—do take place, and … the deep stamp of past years … can be eradicated, washed away, and new people can emerge.'

Secondly, you need to think about what you are going to do, and not just what you are going to stop doing. If you intend to lose weight, think about the delicious foods which can become part of your diet, not merely about the delights you have to give up or cut down on. If you want to form better relationships with people, think about the ways in which you can enjoy time together, not merely about being less shy or abrasive, or critical. If you want to get rid of unhelpful influences from the past, think about how you will replace these with positive permissions. Celebrate your successes, and work out how you are going to reward yourself for them. Decide how you might modify your plans, rather than abandon them if they appear not to be working.

Thirdly, you need to put your energy into change and into identifying and using those resources which can help you. Saying 'no, thank you' firmly to a piece of cake, or extra work, or another drink, is a better use of energy than the wavering 'only a small piece' or 'just this once' or 'I shouldn't really'.

Your major resource for making changes is yourself—your own commitment, energy, creativity, and untapped or frozen potential; other resources include family and friends. Tell them what you want to do and get their backup, love and support. If they like you as you are, they may resist the changes you feel you want to make. Or, if you need additional information or support, look for resources outside the family. They do exist, and the voluntary sector in particular has an enormous variety of organisations, groups and information available. If you want to develop new skills, have some fun and meet new people, don't reject local resources. There is an increasing range of leisure activities available which can be fun, informative and a source of local friendships. If you feel you want to sort out more serious emotional problems, you may need to seek some therapy.

Fourthly, change must be wanted by the Child and considered ethical by the Parent. Unless you use the different parts of your personality in an integrated and co-operative way, you will be likely to fail. If the Child does not really want the change, it will find ways of sabotaging your efforts. Equally if the change does not fit in with your Parent values, there will be a sense of discomfort, and the change won't last. You need also to be aware of the impact of change on others, and on the gains and losses for yourself. If you decide to use your natural Child more, your family may not be very keen to take on extra household chores to give you the time you need for new interests. If you decide to be more assertive at work, you may find your

workload is reduced, but that you are involved in more conflicts, and your colleagues may not necessarily like the more
assertive you. If you decide to stop games playing with someone, you may find the other person involved works very hard to
keep you in the game or threatens to end the relationship.

Fifthly, start with simple changes. Be kind to yourself and
be patient if change is slow or faltering. Make sure your
unhelpful controlling Parent is not setting impossible goals for
you. Begin by identifying where the discomfort is. Do you have
difficulty in accepting the positive attention and recognition
you get from others? Do you feel that you never have any time
for yourself, and that you are always at other people's beck and
call? Do you find that you get into a lot of crossed lines in your
communication, or that you use ulterior transactions with others? Do you still replay unhelpful messages from the past to
stop you living fully in the present? Once you have found a
focus, you can use the exercises in this and other books to help
you identify ways of making changes.

Finally, change may or may not be dramatic. You may
want to make major changes in your lifestyle, but even these
normally begin with small steps. Change is just as often about
shifts in attitudes or beliefs, or about becoming aware of a
range of options rather than feeling you don't have any choices,
or about minor adjustments in relationships rather than major
upheavals. Usually, if there is a change in any one aspect of
your feelings, attitudes or behaviours, there will be a sort of
ripple effect and the other aspects will change. If you develop
greater self-confidence, you can behave more assertively.
Equally, if you develop assertiveness skills, you are likely to
feel more self-confident as you practise them successfully. It is
very much a chicken and egg situation and different people will
choose different starting points depending on temperament,
available opportunities and so on. It is important to realise that
if you are unhappy about some aspect of your life in which
other people are involved, you cannot change them but you can
make changes to *yourself*, and these changes may in turn
influence *them*.

Making Changes

You may decide that you will stop worrying about your big nose or your fear of flying, or that you will emigrate, rather than just talk about it. You may decide that you will give up a safe job to become self-employed at something you've always wanted to do, or that you will end a relationship which has been unhappy and gamey for a long time. You may take up jazz-dance or aerobics, or join a walking group in order to get more exercise. You may decide to take up tai chi, meditation or relaxation skills in order to feel less stressed. You may decide to change the ways you use your time, or the different parts of your personality so that you have a better sense of being a whole person. You may simply (although this can be the most difficult change of all) decide to change your attitudes so that although a problem doesn't go away, your changed attitude towards it stops it being such a problem to you.

Learning to like yourself warts and all may mean a very real change in your attitude to yourself and your real or imagined failings. Negative feelings, such as guilt, anger and depression use up a good deal of energy, but rarely solve problems; giving up these feelings may mean a real change in your attitudes to yourself, others and any problems you may still have to face. There is increasing evidence that our emotions and attitudes play a part in our general health and well-being. Stress, for example, is thought by some members of the medical profession to be a causative factor in heart attacks and illnesses such as cancer. Changing attitudes, as well as behaviour, may make a very real difference to your physical, as well as your emotional, well-being.

Whether or not you decide to make some changes in your life, the advice in *The Tao of Pooh* [2] is useful when it suggests that:

'There are things about ourselves that we need to get rid of; there are things we need to change. But at the same time, we do not need to be too desperate, too ruthless, too combative. Along the way to usefulness and happiness, many of those things will change themselves, and the others can be worked on as we go. For within...each of us is something special, and that we need to keep.'

Change takes understanding, time, energy, commitment and enthusiasm, as well as a belief that it is possible. Other people can give information, ideas, support, encouragement, or practical help, but they cannot actually solve your problems for you. It can be hard work, but fun as well. It involves you in understanding yourself, as well as discovering what you want to keep and to change. Chapter 11, therefore, consists of some exercises that you can use, both to enhance your understanding of your own and others' behaviour, and as a jumping-off point for making changes.

Help Yourself to Change

All shall be well, and all shall be well and all manner
of things shall be well (Mother Julian of Norwich)

All of the exercises in this chapter have a dual purpose. They flesh out the topics already covered in the earlier chapters and give you a chance to examine your own personality, attitudes and behaviour, and whether or not you want to make any changes. They also provide some ideas about change. The ideas and suggestions given are only examples, intended to trigger off your creativity in finding your own solutions to things you may feel you want to change. Whether you are making internal changes (deciding to like yourself better or to stop driving yourself so hard) or external ones (being more patient or assertive, or spending more time on your friendships), it is important to begin by thinking about the things you want to keep, rather than focusing entirely on the things you want to change.

Making a Contract for Change

The first step in making any change is to make a clear commitment with yourself and, perhaps, others about what you want and how you will go about it. This will help you to find out how committed you are to change, and what support, if any, you are likely to get from others. When doing this, remember to start with small, achievable steps (the one day at a time philosophy). If you are breaking habits, you need a lot of energy to do so, as giving them up will require additional inputs of energy if you are to break the old pattern and establish the new one. Make sure that you are picking a good time for change, and be aware of the gains and losses there might be for you and others. Begin by asking yourself the following questions:

1. What do you want to change/achieve? Is it ethical (that is, acceptable to your Parent), attainable (agreed by your Adult that it is a feasible change) and wanted (your Child will really have to want the change, otherwise you won't find you have the energy you need for change)? Have you considered the impact of change on both yourself and others who might be affected? Have you set your sights on small changes, as well as grand designs, so that you can celebrate small and immediate, as well as large and long-term successes?

The answers to these questions give you the goal you are working towards, and help you to break it down into manageable proportions.

2. What do you need to do to achieve the goal? Do you need more information or resources? Do you need to change aspects of your attitudes, behaviour or feelings?

The answers to these questions help you to identify specific things you need to do differently if the changes are to be successful.

3. What are you willing to do to achieve the goal? Are there any differences between what you are willing to do and what you need to do? If so, how can you sort these out?

The answers to these questions help you examine the energy and motivation you have available for change. You may find that you think you want to change, but that you are not ready, for whatever reason, to do the things you need to do to achieve it. You may also find that you have set goals that are not feasible or attainable at present.

4. How will other people help or possibly hinder you in your efforts to reach your goal? Are you aware of the impact of your changes on others? Are you willing to accept these?

The answers to these questions help you to identify sources of support, as well as people who might try to sabotage your efforts.

5. How will you know when you have reached your goal?

The answer to this question helps you to be very clear and specific about what you want to achieve, and prevents vague, unattainable goals.

6. Finally, how are you likely to sabotage yourself?

The answer to this question helps you to identify attitudes, beliefs and behaviours that may interfere with the achievement of the goal. If they exist, you may need to tackle them first.

In deciding how to make changes, it is important to concentrate on things you will do, as much as (if not more than) things you will stop doing. If you decide to stop smoking, for example, what pleasurable things can you take up instead? If you decide to stop driving yourself so hard at work, what enjoyable ways can you find to spend the time you have saved?

The exercises that follow are based on each of the earlier chapters of this book. You may decide to look at them in order, or to begin with the aspect of yourself you most want to change. However, as one aspect of personality and behaviour inevitably has impacts on others, you may find that there is some overlap in the exercises or that what you find in one exercise leads you naturally towards looking at other aspects of yourself.

EXERCISE 1. Understanding Your Attention/Recognition Pattern

In order to understand your own particular attention/recognition pattern, think about the following in relation to people with whom you come into contact.

1. *Giving positive recognition and attention*
Do you tell your family and friends about your affection for them, and show them how much you value and appreciate

them, or do you tend to assume they know, and you don't need to remind them? Are you generous with praise about a job well done, or your pleasure in others' successes, or do you tend to feel embarrassed about showing your feelings, thinking that people won't believe you, or will take advantage of you or that too much praise and attention will make people arrogant?

2. *Giving constructive criticism*

Are you able to give positive feedback about things that, in your view, do need some changes. Does it include how people can change? Is it really information that is good for the person receiving it? Or do you, because you fear conflict, fail to give any criticism at all, letting people know indirectly by being moody, resentful or martyred?

3. *Giving negative recognition and attention*

Do you believe that telling people your positive feelings for them is not generally a good thing, preferring to give mainly negative or non-constructive attention to them? Perhaps you only comment when a job hasn't been very well done, or, when discussing people, tend to pull them to pieces, rather than talk about their good qualities.

4. *Receiving and accepting positive recognition from others*

Do you receive the positive recognition you feel you deserve? If you don't, perhaps it is because you live or work in an environment in which people only tend to comment on the things they don't like, rather than the things they do like. Do you in fact receive plenty of positive recognition, but find difficulty in accepting it?

There are several methods by which you can discount positive recognition and attention thereby ensuring that, somehow, you always find the sting in the tail. Check to see whether you use any of the following ways of ensuring that you don't actually accept the positive recognition you are given.

(a) You can discount a remark about a pretty dress or a smart shirt you're wearing by a comment such as 'Oh, it's only an old one I just threw on in a hurry'.

(b) When your boss tells you what a good job you've done by getting record sales figures for the month, you can tell yourself she didn't mean it by thinking to yourself 'Hmm ... wonder what she's after?'

(c) When you're told a piece of work you've completed is first-rate, you can tell yourself the other person doesn't know what he's talking about by thinking 'What does he know about it anyway?'

(d) When you're told how nice the decorating you've just finished looks, you can tone it down, or neutralise it by comments such as 'We ... ll, I suppose it's alright, if you don't look at it too closely'.

(e) When a friend thanks you for a meal she's enjoyed, you can reject it by feeling that she should have said something much better, such as 'That was the best meal I've had in years'.

(f) When someone says 'I love you', you can pay for it by feeling you must give back as good as you get, so that you always say 'I love you, too', rather than feeling you can just enjoy the comment you have received.

(g) Finally, you can simply ignore the positive recognition you receive.

5. *Receiving constructive criticism*

If you receive constructive criticism, are you willing to discuss it and to learn from it, or do you get defensive, angry or upset? If you've had several glasses of wine at a party, and you're supposed to be driving home, would you respond to 'Don't forget you're driving home' with 'I know—I'm sticking to soft drinks now' or would you say 'Don't be a wet blanket, always trying to spoil my fun'.

6. *Receiving negative recognition and attention*

If you are given negative recognition, do you accept it with open arms, adding some of your own for good measure? Or are you able to reject it, so that you respond to the comment 'what a gaudy dress' with 'Oh, do you think so? I've decided to wear brighter colours and I like it'.

7. *Asking for positive recognition and attention*

Are you able to ask for positive attention when you feel you need it from others—for feedback on your work, your appearance, for a hug or for someone simply to listen while you tell them about a problem? If you don't get the attention you've asked for, are you able to find ways of taking care of your own needs, or do you feel that, yet again, your expectations of people have been shattered?

8. *Giving yourself positive and negative recognition*

Are you well able to give yourself positive recognition, and to value yourself as a good enough person? Are you good at taking care of yourself, relaxing when you are tired, eating well, but sensibly, taking some exercise, having some fun, reminding yourself about the things you like about yourself and do well? Or do you tend to be very critical of yourself, spending much of your time castigating yourself for what you see as your faults and failings?

9. *Making changes*

If you decide you would like to make some changes, you can begin to do so by becoming aware of the good qualities you do possess, by accepting, rather than rejecting or re-interpreting the positive feedback you get from others, by being kinder to yourself and learning to like and value yourself, even with what you see as your imperfections. Initially, at least, it can feel rather difficult simply to say 'Thank you' if someone tells you you look nice, but as you begin really to accept the positive feedback you get from others, you will find you are changing your view of yourself.

If you tend to have a negative view of yourself, you can begin to change this by becoming aware of the positive qualities you possess in terms of your personality, skills, and talents. For example, you could make a list of all the things you like and value about yourself. Maybe you could show it to some people you are close to, and get their views as well. If they add things to the list, make sure that you really hear and accept what they say. If you find that you have ways of re-interpreting or discounting positive attention from others, this exercise could give you an opportunity to begin to change that pattern.

If you work or live in an environment which is negative and unrewarding, you may be able to think of ways of making it happier for you—meeting friends for lunch if your working environment isn't very happy, finding ways of reducing the boring tasks at home so that you can spend more time doing the things you enjoy. Perhaps you can begin to give more positive feedback to others, and to look for people's good qualities, rather than concentrating on their faults. You may need to value your own good qualities more, and be more open and assertive in meeting your own needs.

You may feel that a relationship you once enjoyed is no longer a very happy one. We can expect so much from our relationships that, in our dissatisfaction with what isn't there, we sometimes lose sight of the qualities that still exist. Perhaps you can become more aware of the good things still remaining. Or you may find that caring for your children, or dealing with pressures at work mean that you haven't spent a relaxed evening with your partner for a very long time. Perhaps you can find a baby-sitter so that you can go out, or you can plan a relaxed evening together at home over a special meal.

You may even need to consider putting your energy into making more drastic changes, such as changing jobs, or ending a relationship, with as little hurt to yourself and others as possible.

EXERCISE 2. Understanding the *Child*

In order to get a better understanding of your Child, think about how you use the following parts of your personality:

1. *The positive natural Child*
What did you enjoy most when you were younger, or before work got so hectic? There may be interests you can redevelop, or things you've always thought you would like to do, if only you had time ... money ... less to worry about. If there are, how can

you find the time and so on to allow you to do some of these things? Can you cut down on the boring jobs you do or get more help from others, or spend less time doing things you feel you ought to do, rather than things you feel you want to do?

2. *The positive adapted Child*

If you lack confidence in making easy and relaxed relationships, or in facing new situations, you could perhaps concentrate on meeting people with whom you have a common interest, so that small talk is easier and may lead to closer friendships, or you could learn deep breathing or relaxation techniques. You may even need to value more completely the close friendships you do have—good relationships are reflected in quality, not in quantity. Or you may have skills and talents you could use to bring you into greater contact with people—teaching people to read and write, helping with the sports training in a youth club, and so on.

3. *The negative natural Child*

If some of your behaviour, even though it seems exciting, is destructive to you, you need to find ways of getting your excitement in more constructive ways, even though they may still have elements of risk—taking up hang-gliding, or sub-aqua, for example. You may also, if your behaviour is seriously destructive to you, need to seek skilled counselling to help you understand yourself and to support you as you make changes in your behaviour and attitudes.

4. *The negative adapted Child*

If you have already made some decisions to enjoy your positive Child more, you should find that, as you do this, your negative Child decreases automatically. You may also need to carry out some of the other exercises in this chapter to help you understand more clearly the source of your unhappy or angry feelings. So if you can begin to find ways, however small, in which you can use the happier part of your Child, you will discover that you are feeling better even though you may not understand the origins of your behaviour.

EXERCISE 3. Using the *Adult* for Problem Solving

The following exercise can help you isolate facts, feelings and opinions, as well as getting you to consider whether any of your feelings or opinions are out of date. Think first of something that you would like to change, and then use the exercise to examine the Parent, Adult and Child components of the problem.

1. *What Parent opinions/values/oughts do you hold?*

Are they are still relevant to your life or are they out-of-date opinions, appropriate perhaps when you first accepted them? Perhaps they were right for your parents, but not really relevant to you. What values and opinions do you hold that are useful to you in considering this problem? If you need some new values, such as being kinder to yourself, what can you do to develop them?

2. *What Adult information do you have?*

You may not have enough information to solve the problem, or you may not be fully aware of the information/ resources/skills you either have access to or possess. Or you may have enough information, but be ignoring it because your feelings or opinions are getting in the way. If so, you may need to get more information, become aware of the resources you have available or of the information you are currently ignoring.

3. *What Child feelings do you have?*

These may also be left-over feelings from childhood, rather than feelings that are relevant to the situation now, or they may be the wrong feelings for the situation—self-blame, when a healthy anger is more appropriate, or depression when sadness is more relevant. You may need to become aware of your real feelings rather than blocking them, as well as realising that, very often, feelings can help you towards correct action. Your Child often knows intuitively what the right or wrong solution is to a problem, but you need to give yourself a chance to hear what your Child is telling you.

4. *What can you do now?*

Having slotted the Child, Adult and Parent into their separate components, now examine the various options open to you, being as imaginative and creative as possible. Next consider the outcome of each option, and finally consider the feelings you have in relation to each option. As your Adult thinking and Child feelings examine the possibilities, your Parent is likely to approve a course of action.

EXERCISE 4. Understanding the *Parent*

In order to get a better understanding of your Parent, think about how you use the following parts of your personality.

1. *The positive nurturing Parent*

If you are not very good at taking care of others, you might develop your ability to listen to problems, and to give time and any skills you might have to help resolve them. You might also show your concern with words and gestures of affection by giving someone a hug or holding their hand when they are distressed, writing a letter or sending flowers to someone who is ill, giving a hand with the chores, offering your time just to listen as someone mulls over a worry, or while your partner discusses a difficult issue at work. Using your nurturing Parent well involves a mixture of a genuine concern for others, time, empathy, and a willingness to let people find their own solutions to problems.

If you are not very good at taking care of yourself, but are good at taking care of others, you may be able to transfer some of your skill in caring for others to yourself. Instead of urging others to 'take it easy', 'give yourself a treat' or 'leave the ironing/fixing the car until tomorrow', you could begin to take your own advice. You might relax when you are tired, have a bath, read a good book or go to bed early instead of clearing your 'in' tray or finishing your ironing. You could also learn to accept being on the receiving as well as the giving end of help when you need it. You may at first find it difficult to relax or to give yourself Child treats, but as you balance the needs of others more equally with your own, it should enhance both your life and the lives of people with whom you are closely involved. If you are not very good at taking care of either yourself or others, you will need to use any new skills you develop on both yourself and others.

2. *The negative nurturing Parent*

If you over-use your nurturing Parent, it will be important, when making changes, not to throw the baby out with the bath-water, as your ability to be lovingly concerned about others is probably a very valuable and positive part of your personality. However, if you have a tendency to smother people with help, you may find you need to set clearer limits about how much time and energy for this you genuinely have. You may need to learn to say 'no' sometimes, and to become more assertive about your own needs. You could learn to pause before being the first to offer help, letting someone else take on making the tea at the cricket match, doing the extra accounts or becoming the secretary of the school festival for yet another year.

I am not, in any way, suggesting you stop being helpful, or give up all those tasks which enable so many of our voluntary and helping agencies to run so well. What I am suggesting is that if, because of your other commitments, you take on these jobs with a sinking heart, or feel that the demands of others are draining you of energy and enthusiasm, then a reassessment of your nurturing Parent might be useful.

3. *The positive controlling Parent*

If you tend to be afraid of conflict or of offending or upsetting people, you may find it difficult, when you are faced with the responsibility of setting limits or giving critical feedback, to do so in a positive way. You may need to develop the ability to be assertive (which is very different from being aggressive), so that you can (among other things) give people information and instructions clearly, take back faulty goods without sounding as though you are to blame for the fault, or involve your children in household chores, even though they are unlikely to want to do them.

If you find it difficult to set positive limits on your own behaviour you may find you eat, drink or smoke too much, or find it difficult to switch off from work or household chores and to relax and enjoy yourself. You may need to work out, in co-operation with your Child, ways of cutting down (or giving up) the harmful pleasures you enjoy, and of finding other pleasures instead. If you are a smoker, or a chocolate addict, or a real ale person, you may find that nothing else gives quite the same pleasure. However, the improved ability to smell and taste things, to find you can get into a smaller size in clothes, or that you can walk up hills without getting so puffed out may prove themselves just as pleasurable, once given the chance. If you find that life is all work and no play, then you will need, again in co-operation with the Child, to discover that, essential though you may be to your firm or family, you can in fact cut down on some things and cut out others altogether. You will also find you can delegate more, so enabling you to find more time for Child fun, enjoyment and creativity.

4. The negative controlling Parent

If you find it difficult not to be in control, you may need to practise the art of delegation, and to give other people credit for being efficient and competent in their work, or you may need to hold back on your organisational skills, so that other people can take on some of the work. If you find that you tend to criticise others very readily, you could practise counting to ten before saying something and thinking, while you are counting, about the positive qualities in the person or situation.

Concentrating on the positives in situations (the bottle is half full, rather than half empty philosophy) can be more pleasant for people on the receiving end, and also feel good to you. There are indeed many things to be critical of in the world in which we live, and I am not for a moment suggesting a diminution of concern about issues such as poverty, famine or nuclear war. It is also important not to lose sight of the efforts being made by some individuals and groups to make the world a safer, more caring place. Perhaps, for every letter that is written to newspapers or individuals about things that are wrong with the world, a letter should also be written to someone who is doing a good job.

If you are very critical of yourself, you may find it much harder to begin to make changes, as you may not believe that you can change or are worth changing. Again, you need the co-operation of the Child, so that you can begin to discover the qualities that make up the lovable, likeable, valuable part of your personality. Find out from other people what they like about you and make sure you accept their comments, or make a list of the qualities you like in yourself. If there is something you really do feel is spoiling you, put all your energy into dealing with that, even if you need outside help, such as a support group, or your family's backup, to help you tackle the problem.

EXERCISE 5. Understanding Communication

Understanding communication means being aware of which part of the personality you and others use when you talk to each other. Ask yourself whether you use a flexible range of open transactions with others. If not, do you re-interpret what is said to you, so that you can end up feeling bad about yourself, or do you tend to use a contaminated Adult? Do you use ulterior transactions because you fear confict, or hurting people?

In order to recognise Parent, Adult and Child in use, practise analysing conversations you hear—on trains or buses, in films or documentaries, on the news or in television advertisements. Listen carefully to your own transactions with others and be honest with yourself. Are you really using Adult when you comment on how your partner has done the housework, or is there a hidden critical Parent message?

If you tend to use a rather limited range of transactions with others, you may need to practise using those parts that your energy seldom reaches by listening carefully to what they are saying and responding appropriately, rather than being stuck in a favourite part of your own personality.

If you tend to re-interpret comments in order to reinforce a negative view of yourself, practise hearing, and responding to, people more accurately. If your boss asks for a piece of work by a certain deadline hear it as an Adult request and, if you can't meet it, use your own Adult rather than your adapted Child to say so.

If you tend to contaminate your Adult with Child fears or Parent prejudice, practise distinguishing between them so that you can be aware which part of you is communicating. For example, if you see your doctor because of fears about your health, you can then be clear that you need both information and reassurance. If your communication is muddled, you may only get information or reassurance and go away feeling dissatisfied.

If you tend to use ulterior communication, you need to find out what you are trying to achieve by passing on the real message in hidden form. If you practise being more open with people who care about you, you may find that conflicts and so on can be resolved quite amicably and that your relationship, both with yourself and others, is more fulfilling.

If you are on the receiving end of crossed or ulterior transactions you can listen carefully and then use a range of options, as suggested earlier, to try to avoid getting caught up in a series of negative communications with people.

EXERCISE 6. Understanding Your Script

Having identified some of your script messages in Chapter 8, now think about whether there were any conflicts in the messages you received. Perhaps your mother told you to 'work hard and do your duty', whereas your father told you to 'enjoy yourself and be yourself'. Or you might have had different messages at different times in your childhood. If your parents were happy during your early childhood, but later separated in a bitter manner, you might have received an early message that 'marriage is good', and a later one that 'marriage is a mistake'.

Next think about whether there are any permissions you might have lost sight of or ignored, or whether you might have misunderstood some of the messages you received. You will probably find that as an adult you may well have discarded some of the unhelpful messages you received and you can now cross them off your list.

If your life is still influenced by obsolete or unhelpful messages, you need to give yourself some new permissions which can counteract them. If, for instance, you were taught that you were clumsy and you still see yourself as a clumsy, awkward person, you may, when you actually think about what you do, come to realise that you are not in fact clumsy, you simply believe that you are. Or you might decide that if you are it doesn't matter anyway. Or that if it does, you might want to learn some skills which would encourage a more graceful you to emerge: learning to fence, or to dance, or to practise tai chi.

EXERCISE 7. Getting on with Life

If you feel that you are not getting on with your life, can you begin to identify the source of and reasons for your negative feelings and the ways in which you reinforce them in your current behaviour?

If you want to change your position, so that you can get on with your life, you may need to realise that the beliefs you hold are false and based on misperceptions of earlier messages, or that you may be holding onto past hurts in order to reinforce a negative life position. One of the most successful ways of getting rid of unhelpful messages from the past is to change your behaviour in the present so that you stop reinforcing them.

Although her book deals with depression, Dorothy Rowe's[1] advice can be applied to all the unhelpful life positions. She suggests, amongst other things, that you:

> 'Don't play the "yes, but ..." game; treat yourself kindly; create a peaceful place within yourself; risk putting some trust in yourself and others; discover there is nothing

wrong with seeing the funny side of things; dare to explore new ways of thinking and doing.'

If you are getting on with your life in general, but find that you fail to do this in some aspects of your attitudes or behaviour, think about how you can begin to transfer your skills into these areas. Perhaps you have a lot of tenacity when dealing with pressures and difficulties at work. Can you transfer this to, say, giving up smoking? If you are good at pampering others, can you transfer this to giving yourself some pampering when you are tired? If you think clearly and make good decisions in crises, can you transfer this to those aspects of yourself you want to change, even when not in crises?

EXERCISE 8. Using Your Time

If you feel unhappy with the way you spend your time, how can you alter this? You may, for example, need to learn constructive ways of using time alone. Meditation, yoga, relaxation exercises, having a sauna, swimming, listening to music, walking, and so on, can all be used as ways of unwinding and *being*, rather than *doing*. If you have a busy lifestyle, these can help to prevent stress building up. Alternatively you may feel that you want to cut down on what you see as tedious jobs and spend more time doing the things you enjoy. You may be able to take some short cuts in the housework or to go to work by train rather than coping with the stress of driving, or to find ways of delegating some of your work to others, or to acquire some genuinely labour-saving devices.

EXERCISE 9. Stopping Games

Games are usually played to get needs met in an non-authentic way. If you want something, such as attention or a change in behaviour, from others , you might play the 'if you really cared, you would ...' game from your adapted Child, rather than using Adult or natural Child to ask for what you want. If you play games, you need to identify the underlying needs and seek to find more authentic ways of dealing with these, including, on occasions, meeting these needs yourself, rather than relying solely on other people. If you are on the receiving end of games, you may need to confront the game, to respond to the hidden need, or to ignore it and refuse to play.

Conversely, you may feel that you want to spend more time in authentic relationships with others. You are more likely to find that relationships blossom and become stronger if you work together on a hobby or interest rather than spend the evening in a noisy pub, or if you invite a few friends for supper rather than fifty people to a party. You will also develop closer relationships if you are willing to risk sharing your beliefs, feelings and inner world with others, and if you are willing to give affection freely and openly.

While changes in our behaviour or in the external situation may be necessary if problems are to be resolved, it is often our attitudes and beliefs rather than other factors which give rise to the problems we face. These attitudes and beliefs often stem from unhappinesses or difficulties in our carly lives. Yet it is possible, given a willingness to face old traumas and to put energy and understanding into change, for all to be well with your life.

CHAPTER 12
Conclusions

Any model ... is partial humbug: only a map, and, as
such, a very incomplete representation of reality
(Paschal Baute)

The ideas in this book have been based on a belief in the human potential for growth towards wholeness and emotional health, and in our ability to make changes which encourage that growth. And, although they do provide a simple blueprint for understanding everyday behaviour, they can still only be an incomplete representation of reality.

They are ideas which cannot in themselves resolve the major natural and man-made disasters of the world. Neither can they take away the individual suffering caused by severe ill-health, bereavement, unemployment, poverty, poor living conditions, and so on. But, as many of the problems which face us stem from our inability to trust each other, from difficulties in communication and from negative qualities such as aggression, anger, guilt, ruthless competition, and so on, they can be used to encourage people to discover their positive, trusting, co-operative, loving qualities and potential.

The process of discovery can be daunting but also exciting and fun. It can help us cut the ties that bind us to the past, thus enabling us to live more fully in the present. Being able to live in the present can be like being given a fragile and precious gift, one which we may tend to keep for best and only use occasionally. Or it may seem to be a gift that only people such as poets, philosophers and mystics have. We can all, however, have this gift and the more we use it, the more we shall discover its strength. Philip Toynbee[1] talks about this when he says:

'But now, on this walk, I stopped several times and looked at a single tree as I haven't done for years. ...The tree was there and now, in its own immediate and peculiar right: that tree and no other. And I was acutely here-and-now as I stared at it, unhampered by past or future.'

This book has been a brief introduction to transactional analysis and to understanding behaviour and personality. Many other books, using this and similar approaches have been published and the further reading list gives some of the more readily available texts on transactional analysis.

I will leave the final word (almost) to Kahlil Gibran[2] who says:

'The person who is limited in heart and thought is inclined to love that which is limited in life.'

While there are limits on all of us, we too often limit ourselves by outmoded ideas and beliefs. If we can begin to understand our behaviour and attitudes, and to appreciate the influence of the past on the present, we can free ourselves to make both ourselves and the world a happier place. It takes time, but both the journey and the destination can be a part of the process of understanding and change.

References

Chapter 1
1. The idea of the 'good enough' person has been adapted from D. W. Winnicott, who coined the phrase 'good enough' parenting. See Winnicott, D. W. (1958) *Collected Papers: Through Paediatrics to Psycho-Analysis*. Tavistock Publications.

Chapter 3
1. Lewis, C. S. (1982) *The Screwtape Letters*. Fount.

Chapter 7
1. See: Berne, E. (1975) *What Do You Say After You Say Hello?* Corgi.
2. Huxley, E. (1962) *Flame Trees of Thika*. Penguin.

Chapter 8
1. Hughes, G. (1984) *The Hawthorn Goddess*. Chatto & Windus.
2. Smith, S. (1975) 'Not waving but drowning' from *Collected Poems*. Allen Lane 1975.

Chapter 10
1. Gardam, J. (1986) *Crusoe's Daughter*. Sphere.
2. Hoff, B. (1984) *The Tao of Pooh*. Methuen.

Chapter 11
1. Rowe, D. (1989) *Depression: The Way Out of Your Prison*. Routledge.

Chapter 12
1. Toynbee, P. (1982) *Part of a Journey*. Fount.
2. Sherfan, A. D. (ed.) (1979) *A Third Treasury of Kahlil Gibran*. Castle.

Glossary

Throughout the text, some of the conventions of transactional analysis vocabulary have been used. Where there are minor differences or amendments, the glossary gives the traditional transactional words and links them with the words used in the text.

Chapter 2. Attention Please

Stroke—a unit of recognition and attention, verbal or non-verbal, given by others or by oneself. Strokes are of five main kinds: positive unconditional, positive conditional, negative unconditional, negative conditional and plastic (insincere).

Chapter 3. The Child is Father of the Man

There are two models of personality structure—functional, in which how we behave is described, and structural, in which the stages of child development are more fully set out. In this chapter, the focus is on the functional model as this looks at adult functioning, although the concept of the intuitive Child is drawn from the structural model.

Ego states—the parts of the personality referred to as Parent, Adult and Child are called ego states in transactional analysis theory.

Natural Child—sometimes referred to the Free as well as the Natural Child.

Adapted Child—which has both rebellious and compliant elements.

Intuitive Child—the Little Professor or the Adult in the Child.

Both the natural and the adapted Child are seen as being either positive or negative, depending on the feelings and behaviours that are being used.

Chapter 5. Parents are People, Too

Nurturing Parent—the positive nurturing Parent is seen as being 'permission' giving, whereas the negative nurturing Parent is seen as 'rescuing'.

Controlling Parent—the positive controlling Parent is seen as 'protecting', whereas the negative controlling Parent is seen as 'persecuting'.

Chapter 6. The Complete Person

The integrated Adult is seen as having both an ethical element, referred to as ethos (Parent in the Adult), an objective, reality testing element (Adult in the Adult) and a feeling element referred to as pathos (Child in the Adult).

Chapter 7. Only Connect

A verbal exchange between two people or between different parts of the personality internally is called a transaction.

Open communication—usually referred to as a complementary transaction.

Crossed communication—usually referred to as a crossed transaction.

Double level or ulterior communication—usually referred to as an ulterior transaction.

Chapter 8. Your Script gets Written

Permissions—positive messages which can go from both the Parent and Child of the parents to the Parent and Child of the child.

Injunctions—the negative messages from the Child of the parent to the Child of the child.

Counter-injunctions—the negative messages from the Parent of the parent to the Parent of the child.

Program—the messages which show a child how to behave go from the Adult in the parent to the Adult in the child.

Scripts are seen as winning (constructive), banal (playing safe) or losing.

Chapter 9. Spending Your Time

The various attitudes that people take up to self and others are called life positions. The four life positions are:

I'm OK—You're OK
I'm OK—You're not OK
I'm not OK—You're OK
I'm not OK—You're not OK.

The conventional way of looking at time structuring is to see time as being passed in six ways: withdrawal, rituals, pastimes, activities, games and intimacy.

Suggestions for Further Reading.

Berne, E. (1976) *Beyond Games and Scripts*. Grove.

Goulding, R. and M. (1978) *The Power is in the Patient*. TA Press.

Goulding, M. and R. (1979) *Changing Lives Through Redecision Therapy*. Grove.

Haimowitz, M. and N. (1976) *Suffering is Optional*. Haimo Woods Press.

Harris, T. (1973) *I'm OK—You're OK*. Pan.

Harris, T. (1986) *Staying OK*. Pan.

James, M. and Jongeward, D. (1971) *Born to Win*. Addison-Wesley.

Jongeward, D. and Scott, D. (1976) *Women as Winners*. Addison-Wesley.

Paul, N. (1985) *The Right to be You*. Chartwell-Bratt.

Pitman, E. (1984) *Transactional Analysis for Social Workers and Counsellors*. RKP.

Stewart, I. (1989) *Transactional Analysis Counselling in Action*. Sage.

Stewart, I. and Joines, V. (1987) *TA Today*. Lifespace Publishing.

Further details about courses, workshops and training in transactional analysis can be obtained through the Institute of Transactional Analysis, BM Box 4104, London WC1 3XX. Telephone: 071-404-5011.